T0128867

# Travel Like a Millionaire Without Being One

## An Insider's Guide To Fulfilling Your Wildest Travel Dreams

Written with a
German Accent By
**Sigrid Carter**

*Trafford rev. 04/11/2018*

www.trafford.com
North America & international
toll-free: 1 888 232 4444 (USA & Canada)
fax: 812 355 4082

**To Travel is to Live**
-Christian Anderson

Sigrid with pet in Africa

# Greetings to my fellow explorer,

Many times people ask me, "Which one of the many countries you have visited, is your favorite?" My usual answer is, "It depends on my mood." Right this minute I wish to be in landlocked Botswana in the southern part of Africa. Located at latitude 24.65 and longitude 25.91, rivers turn into liquid gold at sunset and stars ever so bright dance on the surface of the lakes along with the eyes of hungry crocodiles. It has the globe's most unique river, the 1056 mile long Okavango, father of over 150,000 islands small and large. It is here that its life ends quietly among its children as its soul evaporates into the air its body seeps into the ground, rather than by joining another body of water. The easiest way to get there is with South African Airlines from Johannesburg, S.A. The first time I visited Botswana, I arrived from J-burg, in a 4 seater Cessna. Strapped into the co-pilot seat, I enjoyed a *herrgöttlichen* view over papyrus-lined waterways and palm-covered islands created by the

Okavango Delta. Approaching our destination, the interesting frontier town of Maun, the gateway of some of Africa's most exciting safaris came into view. I could not take enough pictures of the fascinating town with mysterious white sand streets below me. "Kalahari Desert sand!" My private pilot (PP) explained with a proud smile. By the way, my favorite way to travel is solo with a private connoisseur, such as the pilot. This trick I learned from my husband who on all of his scientific expeditions always hires locals to assist him with his wildlife research.

The moment our small plane touched the ground, something incredibly unique happened. Elephants in uncountable numbers, large and small, ears flying, some trumpeting with excitement, run along with us on both sides of our plane. Botswana, my pilot (by now he is "Jake") tells me, is the home of the highest elephant population. Perhaps because poachers in Botswana are killed on the spot while in neighboring countries poachers get away with only a slap on the hand. Jake educates me, "Elephants are smart. They are not only the largest of all land animals, but they are also the smartest. It pays to have a brains the size of a VW engine. These elephants out here… they know me. Each time I land in Maun they give me an enthusiastic welcome just like this one. I guess it's because I bring them their favorite treat: oranges. Elephants go bananas over oranges."

Oranges? I silently wonder. What about the orange in my backpack I picked up this morning? Perhaps I will feed it to the elephants. Unfortunately, I forget and end up paying for it later that night.[*]

As we crawl out of the plane, Jake unloads several sacks filled with oranges. He tosses the fruits to the hungry elephants and then takes my picture surrounded by his giant friends. Complimenting him, I say, "You have a good eye for a promising action picture." Laughingly, he explains, "I am actually a professional photographer. My pictures have been published in National Geographic. And, I am also a travel writer.

---

[*] Finally I do remember the orange in my backpack. Unfortunately by then it is too late and I am already settled in my luxurious tent with private bath and rugs on the floor. Around midnight a strange noise wakes me up. Scared I listen to a sound the like I never heard before. It comes from the tent's wall. In the soft moonlight, I notice that something huge is brushing against the wall from the outside. Something real large. I am thinking, Elephants? My orange? Slowly I reach for my backpack. At last I find it. Orange in my hand I tiptoe to the exit. Careful not to make any noise I slowly unzip the tent. Then I toss the orange as far as possible away from my tent.

It seems that by meeting you, I have hit gold. Tell me more about your favorite travel experiences."

It was my turn to laugh. "I am a professional traveler. I scout out the best places in the world to inform my clients. In fact, I am here in Africa as a guest of South African Airlines! After reading one of my books, they must have considered it a good investment to invite me."

"Oh," he says, "That is cool! Are you working on a book now?"

"Yes! I am working on a book right now called Travel like a Millionaire without Being One." "Fascinating," Jake smiles and I realize how handsome he is and how much we have in common. He must have read my mind because he says, "Sigrid, you are the first woman in my life that I believe I could marry *enseguida*. Will I at least get a chance to read this book of yours?"

"I am already happily married. However, of course you may read my book." I respond excitedly, "I hope everybody will."

Handsome Jake replies, "What a shame. That's just my luck. Can you promise me something? Promise me you will contact me if things don't work out with your husband. Until then, can you share with me some of your travel secrets?"

"Of course. I would be delighted to! But, for the best results, you must read my book."

"I can hardly wait. In the meantime, tell me. What was your grandest, most impossible dream when you were seven? Eleven? Sixteen or twenty-four?"

He had inspired me to open my heart by allowing him a look into my past. So I took a deep breath and began: "My dream was to see the world. During the endlessly long summer afternoons of a child, I would lay, alone, flat on my back with my hands folded behind my head in the solitude of a German wheat field – hidden by the tussled walls of the summer gold. From my retreat I watched the white fluffy clouds drifting across the blue sky. Some clouds I called England, Italy, and Scandinavia. And when winds ripped England apart, herds of sheep flocked the sky, and I let them graze – in Greece, in Madagascar, in Tasmania... The blue of the sky was my ocean and some of the clouds were islands. The islands were skirted by white, lacy beaches. And I imagined soft, powdery beaches while I lay on top of the hard, thirsty summer soil, of what once upon a time was a moor. The whispers of the wheat I translated into the prickling sound of ocean waves seeping through sand as they were sucked back into the sea.

The world of my dreams constantly lured me. Finally I had to submit. And, when I did, I was amazed. The world of the creator was even more beautiful, and by far more exotic, than my wildest dreams. How could I possibly have imagined a white coral beach like Sapphire Bay or that Moscow in June smells like Lilac and that in Nepal I would take an elephant taxi to the Hotel Tigertops – disembark and step onto the first floor – just a few steps away from my room? How could I have dreamed, that when I would travel through Africa, sleeping in tens that had full service bathrooms, breakfast in bed, and hors d'oeuvre served on silver trays carried by white gloved servants? Or, if I cruised in the Queen Anne suite on the Q E II that my china and bathroom would have my initials on them?

While things around me changed from one season to the next, and the small tree in front of our kitchen window grew taller than the roof, my dream remained the same. Even today (I am still of the Sophia Loren vintage) I still dream of seeing the world.

Only today, after having seen much of this fabulous globe, my dream has fermented into champagne. Today I toast to you, Jake: I want to see the world over and over again."

I pause to watch a smile spread across Jake's face. His eyes beg for more. I continue.

"Lucky me. So far, I have smelled the air of many countries.

The winds of the Tierra del Fuego have brushed my hair; the monsoons of the Himalayas have soothed my skin; the sun of the Andes has blushed my face; the blue bonnets along the Inca trail stood o tall and caressed my waist. And the most extraordinary kisses I have ever received? They came from piranhas playing in the Amazon Basin. Oh yes, I reached out to them; they kissed my hands.

I lost a sandal on top of Huayna Picchu. But that was nothing compared to the late afternoon when I abandoned my sunglasses, leaving them to a tiger. I had placed my glasses in the riverbank sand next to the imprint of a huge tiger paw – which I thought was ever so clever. My intention was to show the enormous size of the paw by comparing it to my glasses. My camera clicked. You will never guess who watched!"

Jake shakes his head in wonderment and curiosity.

"My voice has echoed through the underground churches in Cappadocia where I sang my mother's favorite German hymn, 'Grosser Gott wir loben Dich.'

Fascinated with locations where land ends, I stood in awe at the very tip of the African continent. Tears of emotion warmed my cheeks. This was the place where the blue of the Indian Ocean mingles with the grey of the South Atlantic in a long bowing line.

The most incredible bed I have ever slept in stands under two-story high, carved ceilings in the imperial suite of the Palace. This royal experience was surpassed only by the night I spent under even higher, more majestic covers, those of the star-spangled ceiling of the Sahara Desert.

I touched my arm to make sure I wasn't dreaming when I ate Eggs Benedict seated on an ocean terrace by the pounding Pacific – when suddenly – wowwww – out of nowhere, hundreds, thousands, of orchids floated down from the sky, covering my hair, my dress, my plate, and everything around me.

During most trips I wear my favorite ring. It is a Tibetan saddle ring, an imperfect lapis in a circle silver setting. I bartered it from the leader of a mule train, in the highlands known as 'The top of the World.'

I can never tell the story of my fortieth birthday party with a straight face. My birthday party was held in a teahouse in the shadow of Mount Everest. For two weeks, I trekked with a group of adventurous, friendly guides. They had spoiled me with campfire meals and dances. According to the German custom, the person who celebrates pays. What could be more appropriate than to show my appreciation? On February tenth, it was my turn. But, during the party, I learned that the Sherpas I was buying drinks for were strangers... Do all Orientals look the same to you too?"

Jake laughs, "Just as we Europeans all look the same to Orientals."

"Instant stardom hit me when I dangled from a ski lift 25 feet above Gentleman's Ridge in Aspen, Colorado. All my friends could do was take pictures of me hanging up there expended against the perfectly blue Colorado sky. How great did I look hanging up there in my roommate's voguish ski clothes? What an experience, what a way to learn that I couldn't hang on for more than a few minutes even if my life depended on it. I let go. And like a sack of potatoes I hit the ground. From the valley the ambulance sirens echoed. But that night, at the Red Onion Bar, I danced and signed many photos.

In the spring of '64, the Beatles asked me and three German friends of mine for a date. But in '64, who would've been caught dead dancing with such long haired, spider legged Limeys? Who would've believed they were turning into rising stars?

The postcards I sent range from Timbuktu to the post office of Hell in the Bahamas. My walls are pinned with postcards I never sent because by the time I located a mailbox I had already crossed the border into another country where my stamp was not valid.

One of my un-mailed postcards to a jogging pal reads something like, 'Dear Helga, Yesterday I jogged on an airstrip on Kenya; the day before that in my suite on the Blue Train; but best of all, my run at the Mala Mala game reserve. Can you imagine? My handsome game warden ran with me to keep the lions off.'

Many of my experiences deserve a book of their own. I am trying to keep trip records but I am too busy actually travelling. Seeing the world is still my number one dream.

I just returned from a cruise. On a shore excursion across the Island of St. Maarten a new friend asked me, 'How come you always have such a great time? Here you are – the ship was oversold – you sleep on a sofa and cannot hang up your clothes. You live out of your suitcase...'

I interrupted, asking why she wasted her time on such negative thoughts. Just look at all the thing I have been able to see and learn despite any challenges in my adventures. There are islands, beaches, and streets I got to walk on for the very first time. I experienced things I had never seen before. With my heart filled with all of the beauty I was able to see each day, I slept extremely well – even on a sofa.

Whenever I am on a FAM (Familiarization trips for travel agents), or when I relive my travel experiences while talking to my clients, it dawns on me how lucky I am to see the world over and over again. And too see it as a millionaire would without being one is awesome. Whenever I walk along a beach, sail across a sea, or sleep in a Ritz Carlton, I count my blessings. My dream has turned into my hobby and my hobby into my job. Seeing the world as part of my job adds so much charisma.

It is neat to have a purpose other than pure pleasure while I am on the loose and travel. It is fabulous that at the drop of a hat the whole world is there for me to choose and to unravel.

Seeing the world as a member of the travel industry, on a FAM, is like being treated like a celebrity without having to pay the price. Resorts, cruise ships, tourist boards, and more all go out of their way to make a travel agent's visit as special and exquisite as possible. After all, their business rises and falls with a travel agent's review. Part-time or full-time, a travel agent's job is a dream job. They are dream makers. They make dreams come true not only for others but for themselves as well. In fact, the more dreams they make come true, the more frequently they can travel like a millionaire without paying like one!

Today my summer afternoons are no longer drawn out and lazy. They have shrunk and whisk by much too quickly as I make travel plans for myself and others at E.T. (Envoye Travel) in Lubbock Texas.

And England and the thousands of islands are no longer drifting away from me in the sky. They are now real and bring many wonderful memories to dream about. They are now mine forever. They cannot get lost or break or lose their value and the winds cannot rip them apart."

Jake's gaze begs me to tell him more; however I conclude our conversation, "As you read my book, I hope you realize that whatever it might be – your dream can come true."

# Dedication

I dedicate this book to the countless soldiers who gave their lives in wars to rescue Germany, my home country, from the clasp of Hitler and for giving me the freedom to travel to the many beautiful places in the world they never got to see.

# ACKNOWLEDGEMENTS

First and foremost I want to thank American Express, who, almost 50 years ago invited me into their network. Under their Hallmark, Envoye Travel, the company I started far back in 1971 exploded to 40+ employees and allowed me to meet the giants of my generation. At various annual American Express conferences I had the unique opportunity of being in such noble and most inspiring company as Pope John Paul II, who rescued me from being a self-indulgent fun-planner, to becoming an Envoye of peace, Astronauts Neil Armstrong and Edwin Aldrin the first men to step on the Moon, basketball hero Magic Johnson, Physicist Michio Kaku, Erik Weihenmayer, the blind man who climbed Mount Everest, Aron Ralston, the hiker wo cut of his own hand to free himself from a lonely Utah canyon. Life is a state of mind is what they taught me.

To the tenet of my life: Truth.

I cannot imagine what my life would have been like had not a generous American given me the chance to immigrate to the United States of America.

From the moment I set foot on American soil, its citizens inspired me with one great goal: to show my deep appreciation to my sponsor and the many Americans who welcomed me and allowed me to become a part of their nation. Ever since that moment, I have striven to contribute to the United States and never become a burden to this great country.

Even today, nearly six decades later, I still experience a special moment of gratitude whenever I think back on that selfless person. And when I salute the American Flag when standing in a crowd, I find it almost impossible to join in singing God Bless America, for tears of emotion overcome me while I silently wonder:

Why is it that I am so lucky to live in the United States?
What have I done to deserve living I the greatest nation in the
history of mankind?
Do I do enough to show my appreciation?

I cannot imagine my life without my partner, my very favorite person and husband. His values have made me a better person. His love, honor, trust, honesty, and dignity are the source of my energy and courage.

A heartfelt "thank you" I wish to extend to Envoye Travel's many clients, my co-workers, and my peers in the travel industry – all of whom have been my inspiration.

More than a thousand thanks go to the American Express Net Work for accepting me into their worldwide, famous family in 1972. It was the AMEX ethos that I proudly operated under for 50 years. As an American Express fun planer I changed uncountable ordinary lives into great adventures. Including my own. Thanks to American Express I got to experience such unique occasions as;

* A private audience with the Pope
* A National Geographic Expedition to Antarctica, assisting scientist with their research.
* Breaking the speed of sound while jetting across the stratosphere on board the Concord.
* Witnessing the greatest show on earth, the migration of the Wildebeest in Africa, while gliding in a hot air balloon.
* Thanks to the team at South African Airlines for, after reading this book, inviting me on my first safari in all of Africa and to my complimentary stay at my favorite safari lodge Mala Mala.

And then there is Betty who I am indebted to for as long as I shall live. Dr. Betty Stout who recommended an earlier edition of this book to her students studying tourism at Texas Tech University. For eleven years I was a guest lecturer in her class. The students referred to Travel like a Millionaire as a novel and the most fun and inspiring way to succeed in not only the travel industry but any small business. To quote one student, "This is the only book I will never let anybody borrow."

Special thanks to the team at South African Airlines. After some of them read this book they invited me to explore South Africa, including Mala Mala, one of my most favorite Safari resorts.

Equal thanks are due to Kathleen Latham and Carla McKeown for their help with early versions of this manuscript. A special Dankeschön goes to Jürgen Heise, without whose patience and valued advice in this book would still not be finished. You are my hope – maybe someday my English will be as scholarly as yours.

Thank you Ashley Kilpatrick for assisting me in retrieving the memories that fill this book. Your enthusiasm was the fuel for my dreams.

Special thanks to beautiful Emily Baum, a tower of intelligence, ideas, truth, will, and persistence. She leaves me with no doubt that she will be heard of in the future.

Thank you to Joseph Rangel for his sincere efforts to assist me in editing this book.

Forever I will be indebted to the people of Texas, who, through their own example, demonstrated to me the pleasure that flows from hard work. Through you I have learned that from a life filled with purpose man derives his joy, and from a life filled with guilt man derives his strength.

Thank you again, America, as nothing would have been possible without you. I owe all I am to you.

# Introduction

The travel industry is the most ancient of all enterprises, and travel is as old as mankind. Travel is the food of the mind.

Man has always traveled. He has traveled for commerce, for exploration, to satisfy his curiosity, and to advance his lifestyle.

Everything we have today – our traditions, our languages, our knowledge – we obtained because our ancestors traveled.

Travel activated civilizations in the Americas. It gave us the theory of evolution and brought an incredible variety of food, spices, and herbal medicines from far away soils where they grew to our tables at home. Travel enriched the lives of the Romans with sensuous perfumes from Egypt. Travel has changed our values. It brought down the cost of pepper which during the twelfths century was so valuable that it was counted out pellet by pellet. Naturally, it was available only for the very wealthy until a famous traveler, Marco Polo, opened the sloughs of the spice market, a monopoly that the Arabs were holding then.

One of my favorite stories describes how the word vacation came about. From the past, the winds of time carry words, spoken millenniums ago by an old chief. I'll bet you can hear the chief now. Can you picture him as he rises from his blanket by the campfire and addresses the members of his flock? "It's time to travel. Let's pack up and go on our annual vacation. It's time to vacate this camp. Winter will blow in soon. Let's go to the south. I know a place where trees are heavily loaded with delicious pecans and oysters flourish along shiny ocean shores." The tribe vacates the place for another, and hence the idea of vacation tumbled through the ages. The stem word for vacation is vacate.

Along the way through history, the word vacation picked up all sorts of wonderful feelings: excitement, joy, hope, relaxation, a special time. What do you feel when you hear the sound "vacation"? How often do you think "vacation"? And when you do, doesn't it send a chill down your spine? I am fortunate. I am allowed to think of vacation every day. How come?

Well, several years ago I read "The ultimate success in life is when you achieve earning a living with your hobby." My hobby was vacations. So I became a vacation specialist. My sole preparation was that, as a child, when my friends saw in the clouds drifting against the sky pictures of bears and boots and poodles, I saw images of England, Italy, and Scandinavia. My desire for travel was so strong that it woke me up at night. And I used to lie there wondering: "How can people afford to go on a vacation? Who are those people that fly first class and cruise across oceans? How do they have the time or the money?"

Are you like I am? Do the same questions boggle your mind? Would you love to travel exotic places and do so in grand style?

Chances are, you answered "yes" to these questions, and you probably did so with a slight sigh of resignation.

I used to be just like you. I, too, once thought that being pampered like royalty while being on vacation in foreign lands was, at least for me, utopian at best.

Well, it is about time that you forgot all these wrong preconceptions and realized your true potential: Yes, you too can travel like a millionaire – and you don't even have to be one!

And you know why? Because I found the secret. I travel in grand style.

* * * *

Let me introduce myself: My name is Sigrid, and I not only have the time to travel, but many times I travel in the style of a millionaire.

The first of my travel agent experiences began with the magic of the mountains, winter, and snow. That is especially true for a passionate skier like I am. I had already skied the Andes at 18,000 feet, Mount Cook in New Zealand, Aspen, Taos, Stowe, and Sun Valley. Now I had the fever for my native European Alps – Switzerland in particular.

We lived in Bryan Texas at that time. So, I went to the nearest Travel Agency for help. Politely the all-inspiring travel counselor volunteered, "Of course madam, there is always the opportunity to inspire 15 people to travel with you and then you can travel FREE." The cost for Zermatt and St. Moritz was deflating.

To find 15 people in sunny South Texas, where skiing means water skiing on a warm lake or on the ocean, seemed like a big challenge. But, what did I have to lose?

The first person I tried to infect with my fever was a cowboy, who after my spill pushed his face into his hat and said, "Me willing to pay several thousand dollars to fly to Switzerland and freeze my butt off? Young lady, you have gotta be kiddin'." For the next 2 weeks, I called every prospect in the telephone register. By February, 245 excited Texans – most of them had never before even stood on skies – landed in Zurich with me.

We had the greatest trip ever. Especially in the Santa Rosa bar where a member of the Houston ski club, who had one glass of Gluehwein too many, got into a brawl over Sam Houston. That reduced the bar by a swinging, beautiful antique glass door... The following Alpenglow (sunrise), police would not let our train leave the Zermatt Rail road station for St. Moritz unless the guilty Texan paid 25,000 Swiss Francs. An hour later, 245 caring Texans, not knowing the exchange rate of Dollars to Swiss Francs, each paid 1,500 Swiss Francs with the remark, "Boy, was it fun to beat a Yank."

And I? Well, I ended up with 245 people ready to travel with me the next winter to ski the tallest mountain in the world when measured from its deep-sea base to summit, Moana Kea, Hawaii on another ski experience on my dream list.

This was my very first experience as a travel agent. Join in
on the fun and see if you can beat me with yours.

How do I get special attention in my travels? Read on to find
the answer to this question – and a whole lot more!

# CHAPTER 1

# LOOK AT IT THIS WAY

*"Happiness is not something you postpone for the future; it is something you design for the present." –Jim Rohn*

The morning breaks early as the sun awakens the unknown, a mysterious environment surrounding me. I find myself drawn into the Great Barrier Reef. Timidly, I start swimming. The river of sunlight is my guide. It leads me into the endless sea of uncountable shades of turquoise. With each breath, I wonder about the secrets of life below me. Wave after wave of gratitude wash over me. In this moment, I feel the strong desire to share this heavenly moment with others. Oh, how glad I am that I made the right decision when I became a travel agent. Travel is as endless as the universe. Travel is the fountain of youth. I plan to drink from it as often as you can. Frequently, the things we highly value we try not to touch and often postpone, hoping to enjoy them later - until later becomes too late.

My friend Irene gave me some lemons she grew in her own backyard in Southern California. She carried them in her suitcase all the way to my home in West Texas. I cherished the fresh lemons so highly that I placed them in the special drawer in our refrigerator with the intention of enjoying them at some time in the future. I looked at them every day, until one day they all had spoiled.

Enjoy Your Dreams Before They Spoil

My lemon story is similar to that of my friend Anne. She loved traveling, but she kept postponing her trips until sometime in the future when she would really have the time. Then, when she had time, she planned to catch up with me in seeing the world.

The day finally came. Annemarie, her youngest daughter, married and, with her, the last one of Anne's children moved away. But by that time, her oldest daughter had gotten a divorce and was moving back home with three small children.

By the time the situation was under control and Anne indeed finally had time to travel, her health was too poor and her energy spent. She was unable to enjoy all the trips she had dreamed of taking.

Choosing Your Destiny

Contrasting the lemon story is that of Doris, who became one of my best travel agents. Anne's destiny was not going to happen to Doris. Just for the heck of it, one afternoon during one of those nasty West Texas sandstorms, Doris joined some of her friends on a visit to a palm reader.

Because the palm reader's office was on a main street in Lubbock, the women parked their car on a narrow side street to avoid being spotted. Their heads covered by large scarves, they sneaked across the street to the door of the palm reader.

Upon entering the dark room, the women saw the tall, skinny, 40-ish lady who invited them in. Her eyes were remarkable – large, somewhat protruding, and definitely purple.

"Contact lenses," Doris whispered to her friends. The palm reader's eyes almost hypnotized Doris. The woman examined Doris' palms. When she finally talked, her voice was very authoritative. Her prophesies were extraordinary and mind boggling.

"You will see the whole world," she said. "You will see the world like a millionaire. You will fly first class and stay in the finest hotels." Doris could not believe the prediction.

"See for yourself," the palm reader assured Doris. "Walk around me and look into my crystal ball. See all the lights?"

Doris stared at the sparkling lights shining mysteriously in the crystal ball. The message they reflected was clear: the twinkling lights looked exactly like the white and green and red lights of a city viewed from an airplane flying overhead.

However, unlike Anne who always had the money to travel, Doris had no money for travel. But, the predictions were so fantastic, that Doris could not forget them. In fact, she wanted them to be true so much that she started to breathe faith into the prophesy. Possibly, Doris' mind unconsciously began to make decisions that eventually led to the palm reader's prediction coming true.

Taking Action

Doris secretly indulged in a new dream. Some day she would become a full-fledged registered travel agent. She did not discuss her intentions with her husband, Robert, because she did not want to worry him about her resigning from a well-paying job. At the time, they needed the money, especially with their sons, John and Chad, entering Texas Tech University.

The day finally came when her sons decided to choose financial independence over parental supervision. They moved out and were on their own.

Finally, now was the time – she wasn't going to postpone her dream of becoming a travel agent any longer.

She called me at the office, early one morning and asked me for an interview. I did not know Doris, but she had a great telephone voice. I suggested that we meet in my office after lunch.

Right before 2 o'clock that afternoon, I bid farewell to some European clients of mine. As I returned through the white marble foyer of the First National Bank, which was located in the same building as my office, I noticed an attractive, well-dressed redhead, walking vivaciously toward the elevators.

Instantly I wished, "Lord, let this person be Doris." I was always thirsty for good, energetic help. When I arrived at my office, there she was. The vivacious redhead. Doris and I had a most enjoyable talk. Then, the conversation turned to realistic business matters. Frankly, I was terribly embarrassed because, at that time, I still hired newcomers to our industry at minimum wage.

Today, I hire new assistants at one-third of their actual personal productivity. Meaning, 33 percent of the commission an agent generates for the company goes back to the agent. An agent has the liberty of drawing a salary.

At any level, however, the amount of the salary must be substantiated by personal productivity. It is a reflection of the commission generated. This is a great system for a person with high personal goals. It is the preferred system by great achievers and a yard stick by which I judge new employees. The new employee who chooses the commission system over the salary system is usually more success-driven.

Doris had zero experience in the travel industry. She was a former Miss West Texas with a high school diploma, and she had worked as an office manager in a dental clinic for 12 years.

The fact that Doris had stayed with one job for 12 years made her a unique and very desirable applicant. It proved that she had discipline and would not run away from problems. I also was greatly impressed by Doris' visual mind. To have a visual mind in our profession is extremely important, for we sell a product that we cannot show. We must be able to create a picture in the client's mind.

I gave Doris my usual test. I asked her for a description of the local Mackenzie Park and the Hilton Hotel. Doris was so descriptive and so enthusiastic. She drew such a desirable picture in my mind of both spots that by the end of her presentation, I had a mouth-watering appetite to visit the park and the hotel.

"She would make an excellent travel agent," I thought again and again. But, she did not know the first thing about the travel industry, and I had no choice. I had to be loyal to my business sense. A trainee's salary at that time was $2.75 per hour.

The expression in Doris' beautiful green eyes was a mirror of her disappointment. "Look at it this way," I said, trying to console her. "You are learning a totally new profession. If you would go to school and study for it, you would have to pay for the learning experience. You would not make a dime for the next three years. If you join us, you are learning at the same time you are earning at least some money."

"Makes sense," Doris said sharply. Momentarily she continued. "Problem is, how am I going to convince my husband? We have not been married for very long. We just bought a new house. Our monthly expenditures have risen to the level of two of us working. I feel a bit unfair telling my husband that I want to quit my well-paying manager's job in order to learn a totally new profession. But, let me discuss it with my husband. I thank you for your time. I'll be back in touch." Doris chuckled the way we all do when we are a bit unnerved.

I sensed great success in Doris' future as a travel agent, and I was tempted for a second to break my company rules and pay her a higher training salary. Then I controlled myself, knowing far too well that there is not such a thing as a company secret. Why, it wouldn't be too long before everybody else would find out about the exception I had made for Doris. Besides, it would be a poor business practice to ask Ursula, my bookkeeper, to keep a secret. Just in time, and still tempted to give in, I remembered the saying: "Don't expect somebody else to keep the secret you cannot keep yourself."

For an instant I watched Doris walk away. She was stunning. "There goes one of my very finest applicants ever," my conscience cried. "Very elegant. Very attractive."

What impressed me most about Doris was her fast, energetic movements and steps. They suggested that she could get more work done than most people. I was tempted to rush after her, but just then a frequent client, accompanied by a person I had not seen in our agency before, walked into our office.

That evening at dinner, Doris' husband, Robert, shouted, "Minimum wage? You are making an excellent salary at your present job as an office manager. Why even consider a job at minimum wage?"

Stand By Your Convictions

Doris temporarily buried her dream. Her husband was right. Minimum wage with her skills? How ridiculous. But her dream of being a travel agent kept creeping into her mind. "That is it," she declared one sunny morning during breakfast. "I have made up my mind. I always wanted to be a travel agent, and I am going to give it a try. I am going to be the best there ever was, and I am going to make money – lots of money."

The way she talked, her tone of voice, the napkin flying across the table, quickly convinced her husband that any further discussion or his disapproval on the subject was irrelevant.

That same day, Doris came back to my travel agency. "Will you still accept me at minimum wage?" she asked me, smiling and chuckling her famous "dee-hee-hee" that I have become so fond of over the years.

"Frankly, I feel real weird doing this, but I have made up my mind," she said. "I am going to be the best there is - and in record time. I know you are the best person in town to teach me how. You are the best in the industry. Everybody knows that."

After our agreement, Doris went to her present job and resigned from a very well-paying position. On her way home, she wondered if, perhaps, she had lost her marbles. Concerned that she might have made the worst decision in her entire life, she felt the tremendous need to be alone - or maybe to be alone with her mother.

Mother always understood everything. But would she understand this one? Giving up a well-paying managerial job to start a minimum wage job at age 46?

Doris' mother was visiting from Abilene. Doris drove to her house. Thank goodness. Robert had not yet returned home from his job as a city councilman. "Moooother?" Doris yelled through the house. The raising of her voice to a question mark at the end of her call indicated: "Where are you?"

Doris rushed into her bedroom kicked off her high heels and relaxed into her pair of sandals.

"Mooother? Come on. I want to go on a ride with you," she yelled again through the house while she was changing from her emerald green silk dress into a pair of shorts and a comfortable tee-shirt. Ruth knew that when her daughter, Doris, invited her to go on a ride she most certainly had something important up her sleeve.

Doris drove with her mother out of Texas and across the border into the neighboring state rightfully referred to as "The Land of Enchantment," one of the few places on earth where clear thoughts come easy – New Mexico.

By the time the two ladies drove back to Texas, Ruth had convinced her daughter that, indeed, she had made a terrible mistake by resigning from her well-paying managerial job to start a new career at minimum wage.

"At age 46, most people show better sense than you do. What is your husband saying to all this?" Ruth asked, shaking her head.

"For once you two are in agreement. He thinks I am nuts," Doris answered. Yet Doris stuck to her decision. She had made up her mind. Even though she invited other opinions, she remained loyal to her decision. Nobody was going to change her mind.

Stubbornly, she convinced herself: "I am going to show them." And, she did. Doris, indeed, at this very moment, is experiencing the world very much like a millionaire. Maybe even better. For many millionaires I know lack the frivolity to pay the prices. Doris, however, pays especially low travel agent prices. And occasionally, she has paid nothing at all or incurred only very minor expenses as a member of a travel agency.

Act Now, Before It's Too Late

As was the case with my friend Anne, people often wait until it is too late to do what they really want to do. Too many of us work in a job that we do not like just because we are unwilling to take a chance.

To be successful in your career, you must take a chance and choose a job you enjoy. I recall the story of a young man who took such a chance. I recall the message it carried because it touched me so deeply. The story was about a young lawyer, who became seriously ill. None of the physicians he consulted could diagnose his weakening illness. As a last resort, the young man was referred to Dr. Bircher-Benner in Zurich, Switzerland. Dr. Bircher-Benner asked the young man if he enjoyed his job.

"Enjoy?" the young man asked with surprise. "It's a job all right. But enjoy it? Who the heck enjoys working?" Dr. Bircher-Benner advised the man to resign from his law practice and start something totally new. Something he might really enjoy doing. The young man decided to become a salesman. His family was shocked, especially at what he wanted to sell – travel.

"Why? All these years of studying, down the drain," his outraged father complained. But the young man loved selling. He became very successful at it and eventually earned a huge fortune. Even more important than money, the young man got well the moment he changed his career.

You Can Do It!

Most likely, once you find the job you enjoy performing, you also will become successful in it. I wonder sometimes: What comes first? The joy of doing a particular job or a job so inspiring that it brings joy in performing it. Another version of the chicken and the egg theory, I guess.

You will find out – like I did – that being a travel agent is both:

It's a job so inspiring that it brings joy in performing it! And, it's the joy of doing a particular job! Just remember, now is the time to make your change to a job you love and to loving your job. Don't wait until it's too late to follow your dream!

Exploring the Brazos River in Texas.

# CHAPTER 2

# THE LIFE OF A TRAVEL AGENT

*"Travelers are the best envoys for peace."* –Pope John Paul II

We were sitting together one morning on the terrace of what was then the Waikoloa Sheraton on the big island of Hawaii. A helicopter had just showered us with hundreds, maybe thousands, of orchids. What a great experience and wonderful surprise – an event I shall never forget. It could happen only at a congress for some very special people: travel agents – American Express Travel Agents.

It was as special an occasion as the private audience with Pope John Paul II we had in Rome several years prior at an American Express meeting. The whole world always wants to show a travel agent its best side. After all, we pretty much determine where the tourist will travel next year. Usually, we are treated like royalty.

Billions of dollars are paid each year in the form of commission to travel agents, and the travel industry is one of the fastest growing industries in the world. This trend will continue as work weeks shorten and increasing numbers of people prefer a travel experience to owning material things. To look into the future and to realize these facts is truly shocking.

Fringe Benefits

Frequently I am asked, "Do you work hard?" I routinely answer, "I never work. I only have fun!" What a wonderful life – the life of a travel agent. I would not take anything for it. Not a Ph.D. in any of the sciences. Nothing.

As we were cruising the Caribbean one year to celebrate the success we had during the year prior, several of us travel agents had gathered under the full moon, pushing together some deck chairs.

Charleen asked with her Dixieland charm, "What is the weirdest thing that ever happened to you as a travel agent?"

Peter volunteered first.

"I flew to Hong Kong not too long ago," he said. "Several hours out of Los Angeles, the guy in front of me, in first class, died."

"Really?" Charleen gasped with excitement. "You are kidding. What happened?"

"Well," Peter continued, "We couldn't very well have a funeral in the sky, you know. But, the flight attendant covered the deceased man with a blanket. Now, the guy next to him complained, asking if they could at least move the dead man to the coach section. Smiling politely the flight attended whispered, 'He paid for first class, you know.'"

Bruce had an equally incredible story to tell.

"I flew on a short flight one day – Lubbock to Houston on Southwest," he said. "We were about halfway into the flight when suddenly a passenger from the back of the plane came to the front.

"In a Spanish accent, I heard him say to the flight attendant, 'The girl next to me is in labor. You must do something. I cannot be of any help. *No puede ayudar*! You understand? No help whatsoever. Understand? You must move her. Or move me.'

"'Sir, the flight is full. Please return to your seat,' the flight attendant told him. Lo and behold, wouldn't you know, the man next to me volunteered to change seats with the girl in labor.

"The flight attendant brought the pregnant girl up to the front and set her right next to me. And, that is exactly where the baby was born – right next to me.

"When we reached Houston, everybody cheered. Somebody had the idea of passing a big Texas hat which, in no time, was full with a welcoming gift for the new citizen."

"That's incredible," Joe said, shaking his head. "I learned how to cut cheese one time when I flew in first class from Paris to Houston. The French nobleman next to me informed me that it made him sick to see how Americans butchered the fine French cheeses. 'Don't they know, that it is a great faux pas to cut from the middle section of a slice of cheese?' he asked me.

"'But, that is the most delicious part.' I told him. 'That is the whole point,' he explained to me. 'You don't serve yourself the part that everyone else is eager to obtain. You slice along the side of a pie-shaped piece of cheese. So you get something of everything - a taste of the inside as well as the corner. Comprende? Oh! Think of a pineapple, the taste of the top taste different than the base of the pineapple.'"

Jean was eager to share her own story.

"I flew on a first class pass one time," she said. "We had one passenger in the first class section that was truly the epitome of spoiled rotten. Nothing was good enough for her. She complained about everything.

By the time the meal was being served, the flight attendant – a charming young lady – had about had it. Of course, the passenger complained about the meal. 'The potato is real bad,' the lady griped. So, the flight attendant picked up the potato from the lady's plate, smiled and, spanking the potato, she said, 'Potato real bad, real bad.'"

The Travel Agent's Life

Although being a travel agent is fun, I like to think that as a travel agent I make a real contribution to the world. That idea was encouraged by Pope John Paul II when he spoke to a group of American Express travel agents. He reminded us that as travel agents, and as travelers, we come in contact with people all over the world. By striving to set a good example of kindness, modesty, respect, and by showing our admiration toward different cultures, we plant the seed for world peace and have not lived in vain, the Pope said. He blessed us as peace makers, and at that moment I changed from a self-serving agent to a meaningful envoy of peace.

Beautiful, isn't it? I frequently have a lump in my throat when I concentrate on the Pope's message. I am not ashamed to admit that occasionally even a tear rolls down my cheek. Do you have a job that you are so passionate about that it could bring tears to your eyes? I have been a travel agent for 50 blissful years, and I continue to have the desire to perform my job as long as I have the good fortune to be able to pick up the phone and help someone.

For dedicated travel agents, the job becomes part of their lives. A travel agent who worked with me claimed that one time she got out of bed in the middle of the night and, in her sleep, crawled underneath her bed.

"What's the matter?" her husband asked her.

"I am looking for a lost ticket coupon," she replied and crawled back into her bed, never waking up. That is about as involved as one can get in a job.

I remember one day when, at 5 p.m., I realized that I still had not eaten my lunch. On a paper plate next to my computer stood a portion of nachos. The guacamole topping already had changed color from an inviting green to a not-so-appetizing dark brown. The bed of originally crisp warm corn chips, by now after standing around for four hours, were cold and soggy. Yet, I picked away with great gusto while I booked someone on a cruise.

When I suddenly had to talk on the phone, I quickly switched all the food in my mouth into one side pocket of my mouth. Every good travel agent knows how to do that.

Sitting in front of my desk on the bench I had constructed out of two-by-fours and then covered with an Ottawallo Carpet, a purchase from an Indian Market in Ecuador, was Lesly, interviewing for a job. I hired Lesly.

How could I not give her a chance? She had already proven herself by showing great patience. She had waited in the office for several hours until I was available.

I offered Lesly some of my nachos, but she declined. Months later, when Lesly was on her way to becoming a great travel agent, she confessed, "Never will I forget your plate of old, crummy looking nachos. I was amazed how anyone could eat cold nachos. And then this morning, as I was making copies of an itinerary, guess what, I ate old, cold brown nachos. They were not only a few hours old. Oh, no. They were yesterday's lunch!"

Lesly added, "It takes the job of a successful travel agent to forget about meal time and to disregard time altogether."

Today worldwide, every 16th person is employed in the travel industry, and I am deeply honored to be a part of one of the most promising, exciting, rewarding industries of the future.

To be a travel agent is not a profession – it is a lifestyle. A wonderful lifestyle!

Sigrid leads 47 pilgrims up the Via Delarosa to Golgotha where Jesus was crucified, now remembered in the church of the Holy Sepulcher, Jerusalem Israel.

Picture by Father Jonathan Phillips.

Jerusalem, July 2010. An overwhelming moment. What a blessing to have the honor of kneeling at the birthplace of Jesus.

# CHAPTER 3

# MY EARLY YEARS

*"Glücklich ist wer vergisst was nicht zu ändern ist."* –Johann Strauss II
*"Happy is he who forget what cannot be changed."*

The year I was born the world was revolutionized. The King of England, Edward VIII, abdicated his throne for the woman he loved. It was the year when the United Kingdom began the world's first public television service. It was the year in which my native Germany hosted the Olympic Games in Berlin, and Nazi Germany showed the world its peaceful facade for the last time.

By the time I was two years old, Nazi troops had goose-stepped into Austria. And when I turned three, the Nazis declared war on Poland and signed a non-aggression treaty with the Soviets. By the time I was five, I had mastered the skill of running as fast as I possibly could for the nearest bomb shelter when the sirens wailed their gut-wrenching warning in my city of Essen. That was also the year I committed a capital crime punishable by death.

During those years I met my first friend Horst Becker. A friend that I will never forget because he was the one who introduced me to the excitement that playing with bombs brought. Unlike most children I knew more about bombs than dolls. There were "crystal" mines which sent glass splinters blasting through the air, fire bombs which sent everything in sight up into flames, and a bomb that thrilled me the most because of its name: "Daisy Cutter". The "Daisy Cutter" was a bomb with scrap metal inside its belly that was released on impact and sliced everything in its path that stood as high as daisies.

But, of all the things that happened that same year I was learning about bomb shelters and bombs, nothing could compare to the two events that shook the world later that year - the Nazis attacked the Soviet Union and declared war on the United States. Two events so horrendous that they altered the history of the entire world and sealed Hitler's fate.

At the age six, I was in a bomb shelter which had received a direct hit. The shelter collapsed as a result of the bomb blasting away the house above. I had the good fortune of crawling out from underneath all the debris. But, before leaving, I picked up a stone and scratched the words "Sigrid lebt" into the wet stone walls of the shelter.

"Sigrid lives!" It was a message we had all learned to leave for frantic parents so they would not continue their search. And, it was an affirmation of life, my life.

The year I was 6 was also the first time I traveled to another country: I traveled to Holland. It marked the beginning of my habit of looking at clouds and discovering images of England, Spain, Japan, and America. My passion to see the world was born. Today, in looking back, after having visited most of the countries in the world, it's easy for me to believe the 20th century psychology that if the person really wants something, the mind subconsciously makes decisions which ultimately lead to the fulfillment of that particular goal. At the time, however, it seemed nothing more than a wish to escape the ravages of the war. But looking back I now realize that I was part of Hitler's chess play. He intended to familiarize the Dutch with the German life style and spread his ideology.

At the start of the next year, the Nazis met at Wannsee to solve their Jewish "problem." In the same year, the Nazis evacuated German women and children to areas less threatened by enemy bombs. My mother Dorethea, my aunt Elli, my cousins Hildegard and Herbert, my baby sister Monika, and I found ourselves all on the back of a crowded open air truck that arrived in the small Dutch town of Ruurlo.

Even during war, nature always has its own plan. In Ruurlo, on Borculoscheweg, front yards were abloom with maybelles. The sweet perfume of cherry blossoms scented the charming home the Nazis had assigned to us.

Across the street from our house stood a tall tree. In the base of its huge trunk was a giant hollow. I set up a market inside the trunk, selling bouquets of wild flowers and later, in summer, cherries from the tree in our backyard. The hollow tree became my personal historical marker, a reminder of my first experience in sales.

As is the fate of all Camelots, soon the advance of the Allied forces forced German mothers and children to flee south abandoning the Netherlands to its rightful owners. We were loaded on trains, packed so tightly that we were forced to enter through the windows and once I was tossed in, my feet never reached the floor. When we arrived we once again used the windows to disembark. There was no way to reach the train's doors or even the bathroom due to the overwhelming crowd.

Our new destination was a small town in Allgaeu in the southern part of Germany where those from the *Rheinländr* were not welcomed. Memmingen sat on a wide plateau that stretched all the way to the snow-covered alps. A sparkling river rushed through the heart of the town.

I remember that every July, during the full moon, the sleepy town awoke with a frenzy for the river festival. The highlight of the festival was the vigorous attempt by every Memminger to "catch" the moon and the largest trout from the ice cold alpine river. Some people used nets attached to long poles. Others jumped right into the river. The winner was crowned the King of the Fishermen and just like a true king he was responsible for the fun, food, and festival of his fishermen.

My new friends convinced me that the purpose of the festival was to fish the moon out of the water. With the moon reflecting on the water, it seemed as likely a purpose for a nighttime festival as any, to a seven year old.

Despite my new friends, the townspeople of Memmingen did not care for newcomers. At every opportunity, they made it clear that we should go back to where we came from. The fact that we were not there by choice, that the Nazis had mandated us to share the town, did not reduce the tension.

After the war, our return north to Essen, the industrial pulse of Germany, was hampered by the lack of transportation in war-torn Germany. So, we lingered on in Memmingen nursing our homesickness for a city that was not as nice as Memmingen, even before the war.

In fact, by that time, Essen lay in ruins, 90 percent destroyed by bombs. But, it was where our memories of home were.

Memmingen will always have a very special place in my heart. It is the treasure chest of my youth, filled with many fine memories and many first time trial and errors.

It was in Memmingen that, for the very first time in my life, I tested man's luring dream of becoming wealthy overnight. I failed miserably. But, in the trying, I gained an experience which today, some 40 years later, I would not trade for any amount of money.

I was twelve years old. At the time, my mother, my two younger sisters, my baby brother, and I all lived on the edge of town in ugly green barracks painted to look like prisoner of war camps so that our "enemies in the sky" would be misled. With men being held in war camps and as the oldest of four children, I was used to helping my mother find food to feed the family.

Although begging was about the only way to obtain food, none of us who begged wanted to be known as beggars. We invented the word "hamstern" which was derived from the hamster, a rodent that collects food in the side pockets of its mouth and carries it to its den.

So, I knocked on farmers' doors, asking for a spoonful of flour, a cup of milk, one egg, or anything they could spare. And, I was the best hamster! None of my envious friends came home with fuller pockets than I did. In fact, I was so successful at begging I was crowned Queen of the Beggars. My coronation was memorable and my crown was made of white flowers that matched my veil made from a parachute that fell from the sky.

During this time, the German Reichsmark was practically worthless. One could not buy anything with the Reichsmark, except a ticket to an old movie for an exorbitant amount. But all of this changed overnight.

On the morning of June 20, 1948, Das Deutsche Wirtschaftswunder (The German Economic Wonder) began its economic reforms. It started the instant that every West German citizen received 40 Deutsche Marks from the new democratic government. Deutsche Mark was the new name of the new money of the New Germany.

My mother had entrusted me with the new money and sent me to the farmers market in town. When I arrived on the town square and saw all the food stalls decorated with pyramids of fruits and vegetables that I had never seen before, I was struck with awe. I did not recognize most of the fruits and vegetables because they had not existed in Germany prior to 1948.

I pinched myself to be woken from what felt like a dream. When I realized that all the wonders before my eyes were as real as they could be, I hung my straw purse, containing the money my mother had given me, on one of the wrought iron posts by the river to rid myself of the extra encumbrance and walked off. (The times were different back then. There was no need to as much as lock our doors.) I marveled, like Alice in Wonderland, as I wandered through all the stalls at the market, taking deep breaths so I could get a better smell of the sweet perfumes from all the different fruits.

Finally I had made my choice. I knew exactly what I was going to buy, something different and special for each member of my family. With my decision made, I hurried back to the wrought iron post to fetch my purse. But what horror I experienced - my straw purse had disappeared! Thieves had arrived with the new Deutsch Marks on June 20th.

I sobbed in pain all the way back home.

My disappointed mother sighed, "Sigrid, in a few years from now, some Germans will be wealthy and some will be poor. I can tell you already now to which group of Germans we will belong."

As usual one disaster leads to another and so I decided to make up for the humiliating loss. Keeping my plans a secret from my mother, I wrote, produced, and advertised a stage play. Being familiar with the term role I figured the only place to write roles was on rolls of the only thing I could come by: toilet paper. Which at the time was tough brown paper. The play was inspired by the fairytale "*Der Kleine Muck.*" I had figured that if I could sell every seat in the theatre, I would make so much money that my family would catch up with the other Germans who still had their 40 Deutsche Marks. According to my plans, my family could still end up among the group of Germans who would one day be wealthy.

I took the greatest precaution so my mother would not discover my plan. (Later, she told me she had wondered why I was so quiet then. Well, I was quiet because working on the play had worn me out.) Even so, a week before the play, my mother nearly stumbled across my secret.

Mother had seen a poster in town, advertising a promising play. The main actress had my name, a coincidence that my mother thought warranted special attention. Since I had been so nice and quiet at home lately, she wanted to take me to the play as a surprise. Once I got over the shock, I somehow managed to convince her to forget about attending the play.

The play was a sell-out. Everyone in town was excited about going to the play because Memmingen only had one movie house, and it only played the same few movies.

As part of the admission to my play, every member of the audience had to bring four pieces of firewood which we fed into the wood-burning stove to heat the theatre. So, after the play, the audience did not want to leave the theatre and brave the harsh winter weather. And, I suppose people wanted to get their money's worth of warmth – especially since they discovered it was just a 20 minutes kid's play.

Our little theatre group had taken in four large cigar boxes full of crisp New Deutsche Marks. It was a lot of money, but we did not see one penny.

We had made the arrangements for hiring the theatre by letter, pretending to be a prominent traveling theatre group from Berlin. So, because we had tricked him, the manager of the theatre kept all the money claiming that we kids had embarrassed him, made him look like an old fool, and probably ruined the reputation of his theatre.

Quietly I sobbed for not having made the money that would have helped my poor family catch back up to the group of Germans who, according to my mother, would have money in a few years. However, I received so many compliments from the people of Memmingen on my acting abilities that, from that moment on, I wanted to become an actress.

I sent a letter to Horst Buchhol, a famous German actor of the time, signed "Sigrid, Ihre zukuenftige Kollegin" (Sigrid, your future colleague). I only received an autographed picture in acknowledgement which I cut in half to share it with my cousin who too had a crush on him.

Of course, there was no earthly way I could pursue an acting career. I could not even pursue a higher education and had to decline the offer of two teachers, Fraulein Richter and Fraulein Bayer, who had volunteered to pay for my education at a boarding school. Unfortunately my family still depended on the food I brought home from begging.

By the time I was 14, we had moved back to Essen and I was looking for a job just like everyone else in town. The demand for jobs far exceeded their availability. We all took whatever jobs we could get and counted our blessings for having one.

I thanked Herr Stahl over and over again for hiring me as an apprentice for his drugstore. Once a week for the next several months, I learned Latin in a school for pharmacists. The other five days I stood in the cold, dark, musty basement underneath the pleasantly warm drugstore.

I spent eight hours, day after day, washing bottles and scratching off old paper labels. But, I used the time well, reciting the Latin names for all the herbs stored in steins decorating the shelves above me in the cozy drugstore.

When things became too cold and wet in the poorly lighted basement, I cheered myself up by singing all the arias from operas and operettas that I knew. After all, I was lucky to have a job at all.

I remember the cellar had great acoustics. At times, my emotions were so deeply touched by the romantic songs and the wonderful sound of my voice that I had tears of self-admiration running down my cheeks. Maybe one day I would become both – a famous actress and opera singer.

During the second stage of my apprenticeship of becoming a druggist, I advanced from bottle washer to bottle filler. This meant that I filled all the spotless bottles with rum and decorated them with labels.

This was my first experience with Pascal's principle of physics. You place the keg of rum on a shelf higher than the bottles you want to fill. Then, if you push one end of a hose into the keg and suck on the opposite end of the hose, the rum will flow freely from the keg to the bottle. But you must be careful and quick to push the end of the hose, from which the rum is now spouting, into one of the empty bottle necks.

My new job caused me a few problems. No matter how hard I tried I kept on swallowing the rum which slowed me down when inserting the hose into the bottle neck. I could not insert the hose into the bottle fast enough without spilling the rum. As the night went on I grew slower and slower. And as a result, after the first few labels, the rest were applied crooked, and some were even upside down.

By the time I got off work in the evenings, I was so drunk that I sometimes had a hard time finding my way back home.

In the mornings, I experienced the symptoms of a bad hangover. Those mornings my mother would apply a wet towel to my forehead while she recited all the names of the neighborhood kids who did not have a job and wanted mine.

"Sigrid," my mother used to encourage me, "be happy to have a job. Remember excuses do not count. Excuses are nothing but an acknowledgement of being inferior. Soon your duties at the drugstore will advance."

Despite these problems, I was still very proud of having a job. But, I began to worry about what an advancement would be like.

One afternoon after work, instead of going home, I went to Uncle Helmut and Aunt Edith's apartment. I arrived with my slip hanging from underneath my skirt and one side of my blouse untucked. I could not have cared less how I looked because I felt even worse.

Edith knew right away why I was visiting them. Edith's intuition was absolutely remarkable. She always knew everything ahead of time, and she was always right, and for that I admired her. She was in her early twenties and more like a friend than my aunt. She was gorgeous, but more importantly, Edith was always very helpful.

"Did you quit your job?" she asked with a chuckle, handing me a big piece of dry dark bread. (Germans believe dry bread soaks up the alcohol inside the stomach.)

"No," I said. "But I am not going back, and that's why I cannot go home."

As we talked, Edith told me about a newspaper paper ad she had seen. Deiter, the most elegant jewelry store in Essen, was looking for an apprentice, someone with a higher education. We decided that, although I had only finished elementary school, I had nothing to lose by asking for the job. And, a job interview at Deiter might be the only time in my life I could set my foot with a purpose into the elegant store.

The interview was so important to me. I felt as if my whole life depended on it.

I did not have anything decent to wear and we did not have the money for anything new. It seemed to me that the fact that I had lost the 40 DM on the day of the birth of the German Economic Miracle had made my mother's prediction come true because we certainly belonged to the poor people of Germany.

But I was not to be deterred. I borrowed a dress from Ingrid Strauss. Ingrid's dress had come out of a Care package from some Quakers in Florida. My mother ironed the dress with great love, prayers, and determination.

When I stood inside the store at Deiter, I looked, and felt, like a princess. The dress was pink cotton with white inserts and a perfect match for the white leather shoes I had borrowed from Marion Kaiser. I knew I looked sophisticated and spoiled rotten, like a wealthy family's only daughter. At least, that's how I felt.

The other dozens of job contenders were all sitting on long benches in the corner of the elegant store. When one of the employees asked me to join the others, I declined. I did not want to sit down because I knew my beautiful dress wrinkled badly. That was also why I had walked for an hour from our apartment to get to the store.

I strolled around the large store, pretending to be Marikka Roeck, my favorite German movie star. Sparked by curiosity, I bowed over the glass of the long display cases. That part was not a pretense: I was totally in awe of the fabulous jewelry before my eyes.

Following the interview, I passed all the beautiful applicants in a cloud of guilt because I had want they were longing for. I was the only one who did not have a higher education. I was the only one overwhelmed by the beauty of the jewelry on display. I was the only one who put the time we waited to good use, learning and observing. And, I was the only one who showed enthusiasm, the natural sales tool.

I could not have dreamed about a finer career. Nor could I have had a finer environment to come to every day. This job opened a whole new world to me that I had no clue existed, a world several steps above what I was accustomed to. An

> Live your life the way you want the world to be

environment I wanted to nurture and contribute to. After all, you live your life the way you want the world to be.

Five years later, after I finished my three-year apprenticeship at Deiter plus two additional years as a sales person, I decided that the path to advancement in my career was by seeing to it that I could converse meaningfully in the four most important languages of the time – English, French, Spanish, and my native German.

Deiter sold jewelry to quite a few tourists and to be able to speak French, English, and Spanish was a distinct advantage. I decided that the fastest way to learn a language was to live and work in the particular country in which the language was spoken.

So, I lived in England, France, and Spain until my task was completed. Most of the time I worked as a domestic, a job which offered the fringe benefit of allowing me to stay in lovely homes, enjoying superb accommodations, learning about gourmet meals, distinguishing accompanying wines, and being subjected to languages spoken by the cream of society. I learned how to be a gracious hostess and to cook Yorkshire Pudding and quiches of all sorts. I gained a fabulous insight into the true culture of each country. And, best of all, I was earning money while learning about the world. All of a sudden a door opened to all the fabulous possibilities in life that came free. I did not pay a penny for this superb education.

When I finally returned to Germany about five years later, the German economy had changed completely. Instead of people looking for jobs, accepting any job they could find, companies now were looking for employees and were hard pressed to find any. The German economy was booming. Everyone was working. Germany approached near full employment of its work force. Unemployment had dropped to a miraculous one percent. Workers had to be imported from abroad so that Italians were building German roads and extending our railroad system.

As homesick as I had been and as much as I had anticipated returning to my native country, something bewildering happened to me when I went home. After two weeks at home, I realized, I was no longer just German. I had become a citizen of the world. I had tasted a small portion of the world outside my own, and I had an incurable appetite to see as much of the world as was humanly possible.

I had outgrown my home town. Deiter did not inspire me anymore. I felt a sense of separation from the friends I had left behind five years earlier, both physically and in terms of experiences. If they only knew how incredibly fabulous it was to live and learn among other cultures!

Austria: Exploring the movie set of the Sound of Music leads to memories of working for the Trapp Family.

During World War II, my family was evacuated into the German Alps and I got to live in the shadow of the fairy tale castle built by King Ludwig II of Bavaria and many snow covered mornings I found my way to school on skies.

# CHAPTER 4

# TO NEW YORK AND BEYOND

*"Success is an uphill climp."*

I remember the year of my arrival in the United States by a world event – the Sputnik. A woman of the world, "wise" and 23, I arrived in New York on the S.S. Waterman. I was so wise, in fact, that I did not know that in America the saying "Come and see us" did not mean anything except as a nice way to say goodbye. Of course, Germans seldom make such a remark because they know it means business.

So, here I was with five dollars in my purse and the address of a family on Long Island who two years earlier in Spain had casually told me, "Come and see us." I was so proud that I finally had made it, even though it did take me two years to get there. I had never lived in a society with easy phone service, nor had I ever owned a phone. We were accustomed to just dropping by at people's homes.

Without telephoning ahead, I stood unannounced in their doorway and by the blank look on Mrs. Scharp's face I could tell she did not remember me. Instantly my hope dropped like a rock in water. Thanks to the rain, Mrs. Scharp invited me in the mansion. "We met in Palma de Mallorca" I chirped. To which she replied "Oh yes! We met in the Mediterranean. Can I offer you a cocktail?" "A cocktail?" I replied, "Yes thank you!" Having never had a cocktail before I expected the tail of a rooster. *What I country* I thought where roosters have tails. To my great surprise the cocktail was a drink as delicious as melted ice cream. Thirsty and hungry, I drank the cocktail in one gulp. To which Mrs. Scharp's responded by serving me several more. She must have realized that my tolerance for alcohol had surpassed because she kindly offered to me to stay the night.

At first to be polite and according to my custom, I declined but secretly I hoped she would repeat her generous offer. Mrs. Scharp repeated her invitation until I "reluctantly" accepted. I stayed for several months. I showed my appreciation by working as hard as any maid to the great satisfaction of Inez, the housekeeper. I will be forever grateful to the gracious Scharp family.

The day I received my U.S. work permit, I was hired by Tiffany's on Fifth Avenue and moved into an apartment on the corner of 81st Street and 3rd Avenue. To be able to afford the rent, I shared the apartment with two other 23-year-old "wise women of the world." My initial reaction to Tiffany's was much the same as my initial reaction to Deiter. I was impressed.

During my time there, Tiffany's still displayed the famous Tiffany diamond. One of my colleagues told me that at one time Marilyn Monroe had desired to purchase the magnificent diamond, but that Tiffany's had declined the sale. The reason, kept secret, was that Miss Monroe did not have the necessary bloodline.

With time I discovered, that in spite of all the glamour at Tiffany's, jewelry did not interest me anymore. In fact, I remember times when a client would approach me, and I thought, "If I have to discuss another Revere Bowl or another key chain, I'll die!"

I did not know until then that boredom could physically hurt. Days passed without a challenge. Time at work crawled by. The clock seemed to slow as I watched it. Time became my enemy, and I stopped learning. It made me feel old and bored and useless.

The one thing that cheered me on through the work week were my memories from the times I had traveled since my arrival in the United States. I had memories of weekends spent along the magnificent coast of Maine where I splashed like a kid in the tidal pools, observing shells and other marine miracles. I never picked up a seashell, but left it in its place to inspire the next stranger.

I remembered stopping at a New England country inn, where fresh clam chowder steamed away in a wrought iron kettle that hung over gentle flames in the fireplace. The ambiance at the inn made a stranger feel at home and welcome. I remembered picking up autumn leaves during a leisurely stroll along a sparkling brook in New Hampshire.

And, it was not just places in the United States that I dreamed about. I dreamed of paying a surprise visit to my family in West Germany - just appearing in the entry door of their third floor apartment one day. I would hear my mother's happy laughter and find out if my brother Guenther had grown taller than I.

My dreams included hiking in the Black Forest, skiing in Zermatt, sailing on the Lago Maggiore, licking the melting ice cream from a waffle cone as I walked in the mist of Le Jet D'Eau in Geneva, the highest fountain in Europe. I wondered what Hawaii was like. Or Nepal?

I pondered if perhaps there was a way a person could see all these wonders of the world and maybe even stay at decent hotels with private bathrooms that offered soap and fancy towels and maybe even a personal shower cap. And, I wondered what those people staying in deluxe hotels did for a living. How could they afford a night's lodging that cost the equivalent of my monthly salary?

I felt the urge to run out of Tiffany's, rushing across Fifth Avenue, cutting though Bergdorf Goodman, dashing into the Plaza Hotel, up the stairs, knocking on a door and saying, "What do you do for a living? How can you afford to stay at this ritzy hotel?"

"To travel like a millionaire without being one" I scribbled on a Tiffany's invoice one day. And then I quickly ran the ballpoint pen through the silly sentence until it was gone like a wonderful dream.

To change careers never occurred to me. It was against my German tradition. In Germany, once you spent several years learning a career, you stayed with it.

Sometimes I have wondered what would have happened had I switched careers then. What would my life be like today had I joined the travel industry then? I will never know.

Well, I decided that, for the time being, the only option I had if I wanted to see more of the world was to save my salary until I had enough money to pay for a bus ride or airline ticket to another city and the first month's rent. I would take a job in a jewelry store in the new city. And, after a year, when I had gotten to know the city and once more had enough money saved, I would travel on. I reasoned that it would take a while, but at least I could see part of this wonderful world.

That is exactly what I did. During the next few years, I lived in the places I wanted to visit. In St. Thomas, I worked for Little Switzerland. In San Francisco, I worked at Gumps. In Hawaii, I was at Conrad's Jeweler.

And, then I arrived in Aspen, Colorado. It was a move that changed my entire life.

During the five-month ski season in Aspen that year, a very special friendship developed between myself and three other young German women with whom I later trekked through Latin America. We had the same background and the same aspirations.

Weeks later we found ourselves hiking through Central America going against the advice of any experienced traveler, and followed the Pacific coast of South America all the way to Tierra del Fuego. Then we pushed north again, making Carnival in Rio de Janeiro. From Belem, we followed the flow of the Amazon and continued on the Rio Negro into Venezuela and crossed the Caribbean to Florida.

Along the way, we were the guests of presidents and Indians. We learned to swim with piranhas. We faced death as we were lost in a fragile dugout canoe that was surrounded by hungry sharks in the Pacific. The high tide washed us up on the west coast of Columbia in the dense jungle of South America.

But, the best thing that happened to me on that entire adventure was meeting my future husband. We were in the Amazon basin where we had joined a scientific expedition specializing in bat research. The leader of the expedition, D. C. Carter, is now my husband.

Today, when those adventurous four German girls get together after having lived our separate lives, we still agree: The year we traveled together through South America has had no equal. (For a deeper look into this story visit my book: "Amazing Women")

My husband D.C. is a biologist. In 1967, when we married, he was teaching at the Department of Wildlife Science at Texas A&M University. We rented a one-bedroom apartment on 29ᵗʰ Street in Bryan, Texas.

We decided on the second-floor apartment because from up there we had a view, a link to nature which we both desired so much. We needed to see the sky and the clouds.

D.C.'s earnings at Texas A&M were only $500 a month, but he did not want me to take a job, being the southern gentlemen he is. After many discussions, he finally agreed that I could work for a maximum of two years. Immediately I dashed to the closest travel agency in town, which happened to be the best, an American Express representative office.

Bob Braley hired me instantly when I told him that I would work free of charge for the 1st month. My promise was that I would work for free to just to show him what I could do.

And, there, in the small town of Bryan, Texas, courtesy of Beverly Braley Travel, I became a travel agent.

Next to being born and then meeting D.C., becoming a travel agent, is the most fabulous thing in my entire life. I still sometimes marvel at fate. Why me? How could I be so lucky? What a fantastic life!

I started at Braley's at minimum wage, $1.65 an hour. Grateful to have the job especially since I had zero experience as a travel agent and my education under Hitler was at best: Comical, I started that afternoon. I spoke four languages and had seen much of the world. But, it did not take me long to realize that I was grossly overpaid at $1.65 an hour. It took me forever just to make a reservation.

One customer wanted to make a reservation to fly to Las Vegas. When I asked her, if she had a date yet she replied, "No, honey. But I sure hope I get one the moment I arrive."

Another time, I answered a phone call and the caller asked, "How much are your airline tickets?" I knew enough about sales to quote the lowest price. "Twenty dollars," I replied.

"I'll be right over," the client said and hung up.

A few minutes later, I stood face to face with the caller. My boss wanted to know if I really had quoted a price to fly to Los Angeles for $20.

However, it was not long before I was able to work out even the most complicated travel plans. There was Dr. Muhammed Rahman. Muhammed (Mo), a devout Muslim, presented me with a greatest mathematical challenge. Whenever I worked out his flight schedule, I had to take into consideration that he had to bow to Mecca five times a day:

once before sunrise, again at mid-morning, mid-afternoon, after sunset, and again late at night. According to his tradition, he had to be on the ground and on a prayer rug.

I faced more challenges than I had ever dreamed of, and while I still hated to look at the clock, now it was because there was not enough time in the day. Frequently I was shocked that it was already 5 or even 6 p.m. How could it be? There was still so much to do before calling it a day. In order to save Bob Braley the overtime, I would go home, wait until all the office lights were out, and sneak back into the office to catch up on my work.

I loved my job. It was the first time in my life that I was involved in something that presented a true never-ending challenge. I realized that it was impossible to learn it all and that kept me interested in the job. The grinding job routine that I had known before would never set in.

It was September when I first started at Beverly Braley Travel. In January I jetted to Switzerland with a group of skiers in my charge. In Zermatt I had a lovely room at the Hotel Mont Cervin, and in St. Moritz I stayed at the famous Palace Hotel. The trip did not cost me anything.

I could not believe my destiny. I suddenly remembered the remark I had written on the invoice at Tiffany's, "To travel like a millionaire without being one." From the look of things, that was exactly what I was beginning to experience.

And, as I selected one of the ski outfits hanging in the antique armoire of my hotel room, I felt the urge to do something crazy just to show my Leader up there how much I appreciated the fact that dreams in life have a way of coming true. So, before sunrise as the snow-covered mountains blushed pink, I opened the bedroom window, cupped my hands around my mouth, and, taking a deep breath, yelled as loud as I could into the new day, "Thank you! *Got Danke schoen!*"

Well, it was a bit unusual, but I just had to say it. I was so happy. I will always believe that I heard an echo of it fading away in the mountains. Shivering from the winter air, I jumped back into bed.

I had never experienced breakfast in bed, and, frankly, I hated even the thought of it. However, I convinced myself that as a good travel agent, I had to be familiar with all the services offered in fine hotels.

Now, I recommend breakfast in bed! I sipped orange juice, even though it looked like tomato juice. The best oranges in the world are red. Referred to in parts of the world as Blood Orange Juice.

One morning I skied the surface of the glacier in Zermatt. Someone skiing close to me pointed out the golden dust on top of the snow and said, "This is sand from the Sahara desert. The wind carries it all the way across the Alps."

There are so many things to learn if one desires to be a first-class travel agent. A first-class travel agent is an agent with a broad array of knowledge, who makes all aspects of travel exciting and a learning experience for those traveling with the agent. To know it all would be like knowing everything there is in this world. What a fabulous challenge I had embarked on.

And, I had a new dream. Someday, I wanted to have my own travel service. But I did not see any possible way for that - at least not as long as we lived in Bryan - because I would not compete against the person who had introduced me to this fabulous industry.

In 1971, D.C. was offered a job as associate dean of the graduate school at Texas Tech University in Lubbock Texas. That August I said good-bye to my mentor Bob Braley. I thanked him for making such a difference in my life. I am forever in debt to him. I gave so little and I learned so much. He taught me how to travel like a millionaire and hang on to my pennies.

I was 35 the last time I saw Bob Braley. He gave me a great piece of advice that I have since tried to follow and to pass on to the people dedicated to learning the travel industry from me, just like I learned the business years ago from Mr. Braley.

Mr. Braley told me, "The order-taker answers the phone. The leader dials out. If you are satisfied with being mediocre, then you are satisfied with intercepting existing travel. If you want success, you must create travel." And, through my years as a travel agent, my daily tasks have remained great privileges.

I protect these daily privileges with the weapons at my disposal such as enthusiasm and a positive attitude. It is a way to assure myself that I will never look at my daily tasks as a price I must pay in order to travel like a millionaire without being one.

It is my belief that this book you will help you achieve the privilege of traveling like a millionaire without being one as well as the privilege of interesting challenges and helping people in one of the most glamourous industries in the world. I wish you as much success as I have had!

I became a travel agent in 1967 and enjoyed the industry until my retirement half a century later.

Sigrid Carter: Author, Traveler, Fun Planner

Sigrid worked as a model in Spain to earn the funds for a ticket to America.

How could it be that when I left Germany I weighed 99 pounds, and then after two weeks of being seasick, I arrived weighing several pounds more? Of course, I didn't realize German pounds were different than American pounds!

# CHAPTER 5

# WINNING TRAITS IN ANY BUSINESS

*"To be a great champion you must believe you are the best.
If you're not, pretend you are."* –Muhammed Ali

In 1971 another impossible dream of mine would become reality. After 5 years of learning the business with Beverly Braley I opened Envoy Travel. My next dream was to become an American Express travel agent just like Beverly Braley. Unlike Mr. Braley who at the time he became an American Express travel agent was rewarded by American Express a Cadillac and a stock in the company, I only received stock in the company, however my true reward was that American Express selected me out of all of my competitors in the Lubbock Area.

I am soon to celebrate my 50th anniversary as a travel agent. I love my job as much or, perhaps, even more than I did on my very first day as a travel agent. It must be true love, I guess. In fact I've started to state my title on my business card as "Fun Planner."

I am a salesperson, all right. But, what an incredible product I am representing.

I am selling Hawaii, a deserted white coral beach in the South Sea, a Nile Cruise, a hot air balloon trip through southern France, an underwater expedition, the Mozart Festival in Salzburg!

Soon to come, perhaps, I will sell a trip into outer space. Reservations already are being accepted! The trip consists of several days of ground training at an astronaut center. This is followed by the highlight – a blast-off into outer space and a return shortly afterwards.

Last time I checked, the trip costs $50,000 and requires a deposit in the amount of $5,000 at the time of booking. The first departure is scheduled tentatively for some time in the 2050s. The whole universe is my product!

At one time I was the owner of 4 travel agencies in West Texas and had the pleasure to work with 42 dedicated employees.

Endure the Beginning, because of my beginnings, I know it is tough. The beginning is a discouraging, ego-deflating experience for everybody.

This is, indeed, a business for self-starters. There is nobody in the office to cheer the new employee on. There might not even be anybody in the office who has the time to say hello.

My advice to you is to: teach yourself and not to rely on others to teach you or to share their knowledge. Follow my example, contact companies whose travel product you plan to sell by going to the source of the information you learn fast. Tell the company of your choice that you want to sell their product and to teach you. Also mention that you are recording their information so at a later time you can listen to it.

One morning, a client visited our office and inquired about a good around-the-world schedule and the air fare. My boss suggested that one of his old-time international professionals would assist the client, but the senior agent was engaged with another client. Lucky for me, the previous day I planned a trip for myself around the world. I called A&K who told me about their private jet around the world. That morning when the gentleman came in looking for his dream trip, I had all the information and was able to please the gentleman. Obviously my information was the most updated in the office and I booked the gentleman and his family. My presentation was outstanding. After all, I had just traveled around the world last night myself. With 1 phone call to A&K I booked the complicated trip.

A travel agent job is so easy to learn and to be successful in if you really go after the information for yourself and go to the source of the information the experts in the destination. Don't be too sensitive; don't get your feelings hurt. There is nobody in the office who has the time to teach you anything. You are on your own.

I remember my first weeks, crawling home at night, my self-assurance in shambles. At the smallest compliment, I jumped up like a puppy dog starving for affection. Was it really me who could make such undignified mistakes and overlook the fact that a traveler loses a day when he crosses the International Date Line on the way to Port Moresby?

It's incredible when I look back today, to think that in the beginning of my travel agency career I had serious doubts about the potential of my survival in this challenging, new industry.

There was the day when I was ready to secede. I went to my boss, Bob Braley. I confessed to him: "Mr. Braley, I cannot do the job." Surprise. Mr. Braley answered my resignation with a pep talk.

"You are one of the best travel agents I have ever come across," Mr. Braley told me, throwing his hands up in the air. "No way am I going to let you resign. You are a real natural."

Thank you, Mr. Braley. Forever I shall appreciate the chance and the much needed courage you gave me then.

Today, I often tell my new agents the story of my debut, hoping to give them courage as well. When I succeed, I see their eyes light up and I feel I have honored Mr. Braley who passed away several years ago.

I wish to be instrumental and open the lock in order to let flow the enormously creative impact he exercised on the travel industry so that it may inspire the younger generation.

As a new agent, you might observe the established agents in the office and see who has the system best adaptable for you. Who among your new colleagues thinks most like you do? You might watch that particular agent and ask if you could do some leg work for that agent in exchange for some basic training.

I know of newcomers who have offered senior agents a tutoring fee in order to learn the business faster. It is important that the new agent realizes that money spent on learning a new job is like going to school in order to learn a new profession, and that, above all, it takes time, patience and effort to lay a foundation.

It takes doing it. And, doing it with enthusiasm!

Enthusiasm: Put This Characteristic at The Top of The List

If I had to pick one quality that leads to success in private life as well as in the work place - whether the task is taking a walk through town, cleaning house, mowing the lawn or being a good friend - it would be enthusiasm.

Enthusiasm makes us attractive, and it leads us to success. It makes sense to work hard at being enthusiastic. When did you try last? Try it right now and keep the spirited attitude in everything that you do from now on.

Without enthusiasm Columbus would not have discovered America. Marco Polo would not have discovered the Far East. George Washington never would have defeated the British.

Enthusiasm is the sun in our life. Having enthusiasm is the difference between having a great life and just surviving. It is more contagious than the flu. Your personal enthusiasm can change your entire environment, and pay the highest of all dividends. Enthusiasm is the finest survival kit, and is a prerequisite of great leaders. You, too, can be a leader if your enthusiasm is of the degree that it inspires others. Enthusiasm is like a bright star during a dark night.

It always gets you where you want to be.


Dedication: Extra Hours Mean Success

Enthusiasm alone will not get the job done, however. When I hire a novice agent who demonstrates particular talent in our field, I let them in on my secret to succeeding in record time - dedication.

And, dedication means working extra hours. During my debut, frequently I would secretly sneak back to the office when I knew everybody was gone for the day. Then, when all alone and undisturbed by the ringing phones, I carefully checked and judged my transactions of the day, making certain that there were no oversights and only customer satisfactions.

To expedite my experience, I would create fictitious trips for myself - San Francisco, New York, a Caribbean cruise, a trip around the world - including all the popular destinations and everything that was advertised in the travel section of the newspaper. The next morning my colleagues were surprised about all the information that I, the newcomer, had.

Bob Braley, my first boss in the travel business, did not pay any overtime and did not want anybody to work more than eight hours a day. But, how can you succeed on eight hours a day? There really is no way.

If you want to be better than the rest and earn more money than the rest, you must be willing to invest more time and energy than the rest.

After overcoming many challenges, my hard work had paid off, and I was on my way to becoming a successful travel agent. However, I did not succeed by doing the minimum required. I put in the hours and reaped the results.

## Think "Positive"

Positive outcomes are the result of positive thoughts. Dedication and positiveness cannot help but be a winning combination in your travel career.

In striving to succeed, take advice only from people whose position in life and accomplishments you find desirable. Don't listen to those individuals who failed at accomplishing their goals, but are good at talking. Take the advice only of those who succeed.

Ask a successful person, "What did you do that made you so successful?" All of the successful people probably have one thing in common: they don't waste time listening to negative comments.

Would I have hiked through South America if I had listened to all the negative comments? Of course not. I could have lost out on the most fantastic year of my life if I had listened to all the negative talk.

People with negative attitudes don't leave footprints in the history of mankind. Many times I have thought of the differences in the attitudes of President Reagan and President Carter. President Reagan inspired me with his positive attitude; President Carter on the other hand, depressed me.

When you have days in the office that seem rougher than others, change the mood and ask your colleagues, "Hey, is there anything I can do for you to make your day more pleasant?" A positive attitude in your life and in your job will bring about positive results.

## You Must "Desire to Succeed"

All of the aforementioned traits can be combined into one general phrase: the desire to succeed! One of my employees, April, learned the hard way that the desire to succeed must be evident to everyone you encounter.

April could not secure the flight a client wanted. Another travel counselor, Paula, also tried and the computer again showed the flight was full. April called the airline because occasionally a flight shows full in the computer when there are only a very few seats available. Paula also called the airline, and the flight was full. Then, the client called the airline and was able to book the flight she wanted at the price she wanted. Such a situation can be aggravating and embarrassing.

April came to me complaining about the airline. "It is not the airline's fault," I told April. "The situation is that the client wanted the seat more than you did, and that's why the client was able to get the seat."

The results that you, as a travel agent or in any other project or profession for that matter, achieve for yourself and for your client depend on your desire. You must have at least the same desire that your client does! You must put forth all effort into a goal if you want to reach it.

A Sense of Humor in Times of Trouble

Although there are many benefits in being a travel agent, I want people who contemplate becoming a travel agent to realize that our days are not spent always raving about luxurious destinations. There are challenges as well, and becoming successful requires that you know how to face challenges head on and deal with them with a good sense of humor.

A test of my own sense of humor came one morning while I was working in my main office downtown. Events occurred that left my South Lubbock branch office suddenly without a manager or a staff.

Now, I probably could have drawn agents from my other two locations, but the managers in both locations were short-handed. It seems as though there are never enough people working in an agency to take care of all the needs.

Fortunately, I enjoy challenges, or at least through the years I have succeeded in convincing myself that I do. I decided to relocate, at least temporarily, to my deserted South Lubbock office.

I took one of my counselors, Doris, with me. Once at the branch office, I hired the first person who happened to walk in complaining that nobody was answering the phone.

"I understand," I said sympathetically to the disgruntled customer. "And I will give a full refund on your airline ticket, if you try to understand my position and if you will occupy the chair I am sitting in right here behind the desk. Would you please, just for the remainder of the day, pretend to be a travel agent? Why, you might even like it."

"What is involved?" the woman asked. "Oh, not very much," I answered as cheerfully as possible. "Just answer the phone on at least the second ring.

"At the same time, hand out this special brochure. Make sure you stamp them very neatly, or, even better, put this sticker with our address on the brochure.

"And, cover up the toll-free number the tour operator printed on it.

"Make a list of all the calls, and be sure to take good notes and be very specific about what the client wants.

"Oh, and please file these tickets in numerical order and be sure that anybody coming in for lost travelers checks doesn't have to wait for more than two minutes.

"P.P. service - pardon me, I mean prompt and polite service - is part of our motto.

"And, whatever you do, please remember that we are a prestigious American Express Representative Office. Sometimes, American Express Headquarters will send special shoppers to their affiliates.

"So, whatever you do, fulfill your job to perfection!" The client accepted my offer. As she was jiggling her chair in to position she looked at me from the side.

"Tell me, did anybody ever do this before?" she asked. "I mean all these things at the same time?"

"Of course," I smiled. "Well, if anybody can, I guess I can, too," she said aggressively.

By eleven a.m., Doris, the client behind the desk whose name we did not have the time to inquire, and I were exploring the office, which was completely unfamiliar to any of us. We had to find airline tickets clients were wanting to pick up, vacation documents, passports, visas, passport pictures and birth certificates.

In short, it seemed that everything that happens during a year in the life of a travel agent was happening to us that very morning. I tried to be as nice as possible, realizing the importance of keeping spirits up.

In the early afternoon, a job applicant walked into the office as I was counseling some clients about a cruise. On my way to the back to pick up some additional brochures, I hired the applicant. All I said was: "You're late for work. Over there is your desk." The new agent's name was Pamela.

Naturally, Pamela did not know the names of the agents working in our other offices. We had one agent from Scandinavia. Her name was Aud (pronounced "odd").

One of the very first phone calls Pamela answered went like this:

Client: "Good day. Are you Aud?"

Pamela: "I never thought about it."

Client: "What do you mean you never thought about it? Are you Aud or not?"

Pamela: "Well, I don't think I'm odd, but if you say I am odd, maybe I am..."

The client then asked to be connected to the manager. I picked up the phone. "Are you the manager?" the client said. "I want to tell you that you have a travel agent working for you...well, she is so...she doesn't even know her own name!"

Finally, at 7 p.m. the very last client left the office, and I heard Doris say, "I don't believe this day. One crisis after another."

The once-upon-a-time client behind the desk asked me, "Pardon me, Sigrid. Is it all right for me to go home now? There is no way I can..." I was scared to hear her finish the sentence. "She is not coming back tomorrow," I thought. I flashed a scary look at the lady whose name I still did not know. I desperately hoped she would return tomorrow. "I have too many things started and in progress. You know, I had a ball. Is it all right with you if I come back tomorrow morning to finish what I started?" she asked. That was eight years ago. Pat still has not yet been able to catch up with her work. She still comes every morning to the office and is the one who turns off the light at night. Of course, at the end of that day, I did not dare ask anybody how they liked their first day in the branch office!

However, throughout the day I kept in mind how important it is to maintain a good sense of humor and continue acting cheerful during the chaotic events. All along I (Sigrid, the actress) was pretending to be Jack Lemmon in the comedy "A Day in the Life of a Travel Agent."

Product Knowledge

A dedicated travel agent is a well-informed travel agent. It is truly amazing what one can learn through research. The best guide book on Puerto Rico was written by a person who had never even been to Puerto Rico. With the money he earned from the book sale, he went to Puerto Rico. And, do you know what he said?

"I am glad I wrote the book before I saw Puerto Rico. I doubt I could have done as good a job after my visit!"

His story taught me that, as a travel agent I could paint a magnificent picture with my imagination even though I have never been to the destination based on research. For travel agents, research includes studying the travel brochures in the office. They are your products. The brochures are written for the public; therefore, they are easy to understand.

Most consumers do not take the time to read the information themselves. That is to your advantage. If you read only a small fraction of all the brochures available on one destination, and if you can repeat that information to the consumer with enthusiasm and in a visual presentation, you are going to be a success. Much time can be saved in dealing with customers if:

a) You have decided which tour operators you want to sell; and
b) You are well-informed and do not have to do a lot of research when a client asks a question.

There is a bulletin board in our office that constantly reminds our counselors of the importance of product knowledge. It hangs - do I really dare tell you where? Well, it hangs where everybody in the office eventually will take an uninterrupted break. Yes, you guessed it. It hangs right across from the toilet.

Some of the inspirations posted for everybody's benefit are: "If we were judged by the percentage we know of the knowledge available, we all would be considered ignorant;"

"Isn't it inspiring to know, that there are individuals who aspire to be the best in the world in whatever they are doing."

And, "Leadership is the unique talent to inspire others to think positive and productive."

Karen was an instant success in my office because she focused on the most popular destinations and taught herself to be very familiar and well versed in them. Karen took my advice and telephoned the sales representatives of several of our preferred suppliers, introducing herself and obtaining instant knowledge of the product they represented, thereby, specializing in their product. Every Sunday, Karen made it a point to read the travel section of several major newspapers: The Dallas Morning News to find travel specials in our area; The Kansas City Star to familiarize herself with Midwest specials; The Los Angeles Times to see what was happening on the West Coast; and, The New York Times to find out about specials on the East Coast. Karen utilized information from around the country to familiarize herself with all the possibilities within those destinations.

Diane was another success story within my office. Diane not only kept a note pad with her at all times but always carried a bright spirt. At parties it was only natural that she was the highlight. After all, everybody enjoyed conversing with a travel agent. Wasn't it fun to talk to someone whose business it was to be informed about resorts in the Rocky Mountain, art galleries in Paris, shows in London and safaris in Africa? Diane made notes about remarks that indicated certain interests in destinations of a particular person. She would then follow up on her conversations by sending a personal note and a brochure on the particular destination in which the person was interested.


Personal Appearance and Communication Skills

Success in selling travel, however, is not built solely on working long hours, having job dedication, keeping a positive outlook and knowing the product. In sales, one must have a cheerful attitude, a nice appearance, and good communication skills.

A good rapport with customers begins with personal appearance. A customer is not going to take seriously the judgement of someone who is dressed in an extreme fashion.

Majority of travelers are relatively conservative. Therefore, a conservative appearance in a travel counselor is a sensible investment.

Personal appearance includes your attitude. If you appear to be confident and friendly, customers will feel at ease with you. Booking a trip should be fun for the traveler. I tell my co-workers over and over again: "The trip takes place at the travel agent's desk." Most clients shop around for a good agent before they put down their money. Usually, the agent who is most fun, informative, flexible, and energetic receives the business.

A successful travel agent must know how to entertain people. For that reason I have always been tempted to hire actors. Actors know how to put on a show. They know how to act enthusiastically, how to interpret places, how to be visual, how to describe and bring to life a beach, a city, a mountain range, a hotel room, a ship, a restaurant, etc.

And, that is what selling is really all about: bringing the product to life! How vividly can you describe the place you are representing or the destination you are trying to sell? How would you rate your performance in the show which can establish you as the best and most knowledgeable travel agent in the world? People will do business with those who they like. Being knowledge able and interesting are key factors in any business.

Practice daily, and it will become natural. The key to success is to act more helpful than anybody else, more efficient and more likeable than anybody else - even on days when you don't feel like it.

It is so easy if you realize that being in control is to pretend that you are in control. You might have to fake it at first, but, if you fake any attribute long enough and diligently enough, it will become second nature to you!

And, if you are the best in your role as a salesperson, your performance will be awarded more than an "Oscar" – you will be awarded a new client! Part of the act includes never giving the impression that you are too busy. Would you select a lawyer, a doctor, or a hairdresser who is too busy to handle your affairs properly and to look after your interest? I most certainly would not.

Attempt daily to master the art of not looking busy through the chaos. It starts when people ask me, "Are you busy?" "Of course I am not busy," is my regular reply.

When things don't come easy and when it takes more effort, always remember: We do not learn from the smooth rides, we only learn from the rough rides.

Discipline and Honor: Ultimately, the Most Important Traits

It is difficult to determine which of the above traits is the most important ingredient in leading a person to personal success in the travel business. Or, could it be other traits - intelligence, discipline, common sense, or patience?

Discipline ranks highest for me, because without the discipline to stay with it, the other traits will not work. But then, maybe the most important characteristic of all is honor. Simply because, with honor comes an inner strength that brings the will to accept any condition.

Without honor, any victory is meaningless and lacks deep down satisfaction. Any person with honor is determined to be self-supporting.


Go Ahead - See the World!

By following the formula for success I have discussed, limited financial funds are no excuse for not indulging in the greatest pleasure of all time: traveling. See the world!

I know. I have done it.

You can do like I do and stay at the world's most deluxe hotels free of charge or at special reduced rates. You, too, can live in the ritziest luxury away from home, even if back home you are near the poverty level. And, many travel agents, especially when they are novices in the travel industry, do not generate the high incomes other industries offer beginners.

The income I generated as a beginner probably would have qualified me for food stamps. But, within three months of my debut, I inspired a group of skiers from Texas to travel to fashionable St. Moritz in Switzerland. That resulted in me flying free from College Station, Texas, to Geneva, Switzerland. I smiled all the way. Although my salary was not so high, in St. Moritz, I stayed at the prestigious Palace Hotel without charge.

There is no other job in the world I would rather practice than that of a travel agent. It is the only job I have ever performed which constantly keeps me stimulated. I cannot, in all good faith, call my job "working." It is all pleasure - even solving occasional problems is fun.

And, it seems all challenges can be solved with creativity. There is nobody in our industry who really knows it all. The only thing that is consistent in our industry is change.

Flights change, cost and the attached conditions change, hotel qualities change, resorts change, politics in foreign countries change, etc. It is a constant challenge to thrive and be well-informed in this changing business. There is nobody who is familiar with all the red lights. But, the light always turns green for the one with endurance and imagination.

A quote I heard says it best: "Don't ever, ever, ever do anything for money. Money should only be looked at as a by-product. Choose a work you really enjoy and be determined to be the very best there is in that particular line of work. Then, money will flow your way."

Remember, nobody ever said success comes easy. That's why success is so wonderful. No client needs an agent with less willpower and determination then the client has himself. If you want to see the world like a millionaire, you must give your clients reason to think the world of you!

Engaging in local pastime of sliding down sandy dunes in the outskirts of Dubai.

Resting after celebrating the sunrise on the summit of the giant Huyna Picchu, watching over Machu Picchu.

# CHAPTER 6

# THE ART OF COMMUNICATION

*"Success is in the presentation."*

Selling is a communication skill. Executed well, it is something of which to be extremely proud. From the time we are born, we practice communication.

From the moment our childhood begins we launch the art of bartering our talents against that for which we long. It takes us hardly any time to catch on to the game: If you keep on trying, you eventually get what you want.

So, keep on trying!

"Determination" it says on the road sign to success. Energy bonded to daring audacity, gilded with the patience to never give up, eventually trickles into victory.

Whether we are lawyers, doctors, artists, plumbers, teachers, philosophers, secretaries, or farmers, we are all in some sort of sales. And, our individual triumphs depend on how well we can communicate our message and market our talents and products to the world around us.

Ideally, each person eventually finds the one product that motivates their flow of energy and sparks their enthusiasm more than any other product did before.

My favorite product is travel. There are not enough hours in each day to satisfy my fascination for the travel industry. There are two major reasons for my interest: the technical aspects of the profession and my love for all the different exotic places in the world.

The first of the two major reasons for my interest in travel is the technical executions of travel - the demanding details, the incredible array of possibilities, the constant pendulum between achievement and crisis, the daily challenge to remain on top of all the changes.

There are never two days the same. Any trip cost you quote your client today - whether it is a super saver, fun fare, advance purchase fare or chicken feed fare – might change tomorrow. Likewise, hotel qualities, resorts, cruise ships and tour packages also change.

The only constant that the travel industry knows is that there is no constant. The feeling of sitting back and relaxing, that feeling of monotonous security, which so many jobs offer, does not exist for travel agents. There is no way to know it all. And there are the daily, almost impossible, battles we fight on behalf of our clients. There is often no time to inform a client of a problem that has evolved. So, we fight for the clients' best interests until finally we win. And, then, we indulge in the enormous emotional high that comes with winning! The successful travel agent knows that, somehow, there is always a way to get what you want.

The other reason that makes selling travel my cup of tea? There isn't anything as exciting as having a constant love affair with all the beautiful places in the world - to think about them daily, to accept their invitation so you may feel and smell and touch them, and, finally, to represent them, to be their ambassador, to be their Envoye.

Even after 50 years of changing ordinary lives into adventures around the world, I still get chills when a client gives me the opportunity to describe the finest coral beach on the Island of St. John, where the white sand is so firm that even the last drop of an ocean wave is crystal clear. My emotions are deeply involved with the products I represent.

It is a most rewarding form of art, indeed, to ignite a client's passion for an unfamiliar place, far away, never visited by the traveler before. And, it is a unique excitement to share with the client the events a particular destination has to offer. The successful travel counselor knows that the trip actually takes place at his desk.

The Keys to Successful Selling

Selling travel is selling an idea. It is so different from selling something the consumer can touch, see or try out. All this makes success in travel far more of a challenge. It is deeply intertwined with the travel agent's verbal skills and enthusiasm.

Travel agents with a natural talent for acting are particularly successful because they know how to breathe life into the picture on a brochure. But, for all agents, it takes practice, and it takes sincere care about the interests of the client.

Be aware of the importance of your vocabulary and your visual expressions. Your tone of voice creates images in your client's mind. Practice so that the last word in a sentence is slightly higher in tone. A high tone at the end of a sentence represents an open, friendly door while a low pitch has something final and can be viewed as offensive.

The successful salesperson knows how to create a positive feeling in the client by employing inspiring verbal and visual expressions.

Instead of asking a client, "May I help you?" start a conversation in a style which eliminates rejection or a negative answer. Approach a client by saying, "Here is our newest brochure on Europe. On page 38 is our best-seller."

And, to a client who is asking about a particular destination, you might ask the intriguing question: "Are you interested in the lowest price or in my favorite package?"

Remember, when clients ask me, "Are you busy," I routinely smile and answer, "I am never too busy." I know, of course, that nobody desires to deal with an agent who already has enough business.

To emphasize the fact that I have time to represent my clients' interests in best possible way, I occasionally call my clients - just to see how they are doing and to find out if they have any questions. These calls have amazing results. I have received additional bookings since suddenly friends were interested in joining the trip.

Keep in mind that there is no better advertisement, no better source for additional business, than the client who is already booked. It is only natural that the enthusiasm of the client will soon inspire others to take a trip as well.


Vocabulary Can Make or Break a Sale

Just one word has the power of making the difference. One word, just like a bullet, can kill a client... Nothing can prove my point of the importance of applying the right vocabulary better than the following disaster:

In my first year in America, I eagerly worked on improving my vocabulary. I lived with a family on Long Island and their housekeeper had a repertoire of very impressive descriptive expressions. One of her "painted words" was the four letter word that starts with an "S" and ends in "T." I wrote this word in my notepad with the explanation "Word of deep regret."

A few months later I was hired as a sales clerk at Tiffany's for their 5th Avenue location. One day, a woman walked up to my counter asking for a Paul Revere sterling silver bowl. Tiffany's was out of the bowl she requested. I returned to the elegant woman, bowed politely and declared, "Sh**, madam, but we are out of the bowl."

Needless to say, the woman's skin turned red underneath her southern plantation hat. The agent next to me disappeared behind the counter, rolling on the floor with laughter. I got an "invitation" to report to the boss's office immediately.

A Good Salesman is Liked by the Clients

Make it your goal to be liked by all of your clients. To be liked by your clients is of particular importance in the travel industry where all products can be purchased for the same price at another agency just a few blocks away from yours. It's how well the client likes you, your communication skills and your determination that will bring the client into your arena.

You can be the most efficient and most knowledgeable agent in your town, but if your client does not like you, you won't get the business. The best possible service is usually the greatest incentive which will motivate the client to award you the business. Consider doing special things for your clients. Put the brochures the client selects in a plastic bag; offer a glass of ice water. Every little thing you do for your client will make you look more outstanding and tie the knot of your relationship just a bit stronger. Several years ago I went to a furniture store. The agent served me a sweet roll on a nice china plate and a cup of coffee. Now, I may not eat sweet rolls or drink coffee, but, nevertheless, the store and the agent are forever engraved in my memory as something very special.

There are several characteristics that have become part of my business ethics: from easy things like remembering the client's name and using it frequently throughout the conversation makes the client feel special to knowing ahead of time which tour operators I prefer to sell lets the client know you know what you are doing.

I offer my client all of the travel aids my firm represents, such as Travelers Cheques and Trip Protection Insurance. Knowing that the upscale client is my best chance for repeat business, I cater to my clients' self-esteem by offering a more deluxe product than he or she inquired about.

My standard phrase, when introducing a deluxe product is: "You will forget the amount of money you spend on the trip, but you will never ever forget the experience for us as long as you live."

Before the client leaves my office, I point out the advantage of securing the travel package by leaving a deposit. It is always easier to cancel a trip than to obtain the space on short notice.

My tradition is to walk a departing client to the front door and open the door for the client. The next day, frequently I will call the client to express my appreciation and to ask if there are any additional questions I could answer. I try staying in touch with my clients, ready to attack any negative notions that might influence a client's decision to travel.

By being loyal to these so easy-to-exercise habits, I have pretty much secured a place among my peers at the top.


Dealing with Hesitant Clients

I caution my agents to be prepared. One of these days they will be confronted with the question of personal safety abroad.

I have a story that blows away any fear of travel. The story concerns a client who almost missed making his dream come true of walking through the streets of Cairo, the home of his ancestors. Being an architect, he also wanted to see the oldest building in the world: The Cheops Pyramid.

He was hesitant until one night something happened that changed his entire life. A pick-up truck driven by an intoxicated driver rammed into and tore apart the outside wall of his bedroom. He called my office the very next morning to book his trip.

Repeat Business

The sale should not end at the point of purchase. Contacting a client immediately after they return from a trip is ideal. A call can take the edge off anything that might have gone wrong on the trip.

Ursula, an excellent associate, plans ahead. She developed a fool-proof technique for staying in touch with clients after a trip, even if she forgot to call the client to inquire how the trip went. When Ursula's plan is in action, the client will call Ursula to thank her for the lovely welcome-home gift she left for them.

On the day a client picks up travel documents, Ursula informs our financial department to mail out on a specific date the small gift she chose. Usually, the gift is mailed just a few days prior to the return date of the trip. This lets the client know that they were in Ursula's thoughts, insuring that the client will think of her the next time they plan a trip.

Obtaining New Accounts

Never stop searching for new ideas. Look for a potential sale in all of your transactions with friends, relatives, and neighbors.

One of the greatest potentials for a sizable sales contract walks almost daily in to your office. People who are trying to sell you something - advertisements or memberships in their organization. These occasions occur with such frequency that finally I decided, there must be a way to turn these situations to my benefit.

I tried out my idea on the next fundraiser who walked through my door. I told the caller that most certainly my firm would make a donation and the size of the donation would depend upon the amount of travel the organization had purchased through our firm over the past 12 months. Although they had not done business with us before, I did earn a commitment for the following year's business.

Recently I received a call from a local chapter of a national organization. They wanted to know if my firm had renewed the membership of one of our employees. By the time our conversation ended, I had a notepad full of dates for group bookings to meetings the organization's members will attend far into the next calendar year.

Next was another organization. Would my firm give the first prize at a social event? Of course I would, provided that the organization would sponsor a group departure for its members and advertise the trip every month in their mail out.

## Know to Whom You Are Selling

Eighty-five percent of travel plans are made by women. Most men do not like to travel. So, remember, when a couple comes into your office, give the woman a helpful hand. She is counting on you to assist her in persuading her husband to take a vacation with her.

I learned a wonderful lesson from Judie, a wonderful coworker. She was trying to secure an air fare for a group traveling to Cancun. The fare the airline had quoted her earlier expired at midnight.

Several travelers in Judie's group missed the deadline. Rather than disappoint the late comers, she was prepared to at least give it a real good try and present the situation to the airline. Maybe there was still a way to ticket at the expired rate. Judie called her local airline representative, but her request was rejected.

So she sat there for a while thinking, "If I take NO for an answer, I will never rise to the top and become the travel agent I want to be... become the best there is!" With that in mind, she called the head office of the airline in question and got the fare she was after.

Never give up. There is always a way. If you cannot get it done, your competitor will go the extra mile and get it done.

## Special Promotions

Everything you sell doesn't have to be a pre-arranged tour package. As a travel agent, you can create special promotions to pull more customers into your office.

Timing is the key to any successful promotion, but so is the knack of qualifying your market. I can't imagine that any travel agent would go through a great expense of marketing a trip to Carnival in Rio de Janeiro to a church group, but I have had agents who asked me to engage in a costly mass-mailing four weeks prior to the departure of a trip.

Successful promotions must be initiated at least six months prior to a proposed trip. The most productive time to promote travel is generally in the fall. Fall is the time when travelers start planning their adventures for the following year. Fall is also the time when the new brochures hit the market.

Now once new brochures arrive, what do you do with the old ones? Throw them away? Of course not! Donate them to schools as free advertising. Not only will they act as a good education tool but they introduce your company's name to the consumer.

The following are a few true life experiences which inspired me in my constant search for excellence. All of the ideas are very successful and have resulted in additional business for the agents who have tested them.

Susan Wood, a colleague of mine, organizes a very successful travel extravaganza every November. She chooses November as the most promising month to promote travel for the coming year because, except for Thanksgiving, November is a pretty bleak month for social events.

Susan Wood's Travel Extravaganza is open to the public. Over the years, Susan's travel show has gained an excellent reputation. Consequently she gets away with charging an admission fee. Susan sends out notices of the event to the market she wishes to inspire, and she encourages her clients to bring friends. She also advertises the event through the general news media.

As active participants in the extravaganza she invites her preferred cruise lines, tour operators, airlines, and tourist offices of several countries. These companies share in the general expense of the travel extravaganza. In addition, they supply the entertainment program and offer attractive door prizes. Several local retail merchants also participate, supplying prizes, too.

The extravaganza is very informative, since it educates the consumer about new prices and a choice of travel products for the coming travel season.

The entertainment is great fun. In the past, Susan even managed to have hula dancers flown in from Hawaii to perform in their native costumes. The German Tourist Office together with Lufthansa Airlines have flown in dancers from Bavaria. The State of Alaska once provided a beautiful stage show produced by several Eskimo dancers who also had flown especially to assist Susan in promoting a cruise to Alaska.

Susan's travel extravaganza usually attracts an average of 2,000 attendees. A show such as Susan's can be held anywhere - from a small community to a larger city. Travel extravaganzas do extremely well in small towns, where local entertainment is minimal. A travel show draws spectators from many small surrounding areas.

Eat and Travel

One night, travel agent Judie had dinner at her favorite Mexican restaurant, Casa Escobar, the other night. As she paid at the cash register, she remarked to the owner, "Do you have a slow night in your restaurant?"

"Yes," he said. "Mondays."

(Judie then) She suggested putting on a Mexican cruise night on Mondays. Her suggestion was well taken, and the owner agreed. Carnival Cruise Line would stage a cruise night on a Monday evening. The cruise line offered to decorate the restaurant with balloons, distribute T-shirts, advertising Carnival Cruise Lines. The cruise line also gave a way a $100 gift certificate redeemable on a future cruise.

For his participation in the event, the restaurant owner received a free cruise for every 15 full-paying passengers who will buy a cruise on the set departure date. The additional benefit to the restaurant was that it was a full house on the Monday night, traditionally not a very popular night for dining out.

This is an excellent way of promoting travel at a minimum cost. It does not cost the travel agency anything, expect for the initial time it demands to set up the event with the restaurant owner and the cruise lines. Everything after the initial arrangement, is left to the cruise line and the restaurant.

Judie did not stop there. She had another extraordinary idea. Judie sent postcards with amazing dream like pictures of extravagant destinations to her clients.

Postcards are one of the best ways to grab your client's attention. They will not feel overwhelmed by words like in a brochure, but instead they will immediately dream about a vacation in the place the post card shows. That is the goal isn't it? To allow your clients to dream and then to make that dream come true.

Creativity: The Source of Sales

Indeed, the travel industry is the most desirable target for those people with an unusual amount of creativity. It also is one of the few sources that delivers almost instant rewards to those who channel their creativity into the promotion of travel.

By investigating almost every aspect of your life for possible sales potential, you can tap markets that may be unnoticed in your area. Check with members of your church to see if they would like you to present travel-related shows on Wednesday nights. Offer to handle the personal travel of your commercial accounts.

Product Knowledge Leads to High Sales

Although you may have a market ready for the big sales pitch, if you do not know your product, your attempt will fail.

An additional advantage of product knowledge is that it saves time in dealing with the client. It eliminates having to engage in research while counseling the client.

Product knowledge increases self-esteem. A knowledgeable agent has greater job satisfaction. In today's travel-hungry society, the chances that your client knows more about a travel destination than you do are brutally real.

So, how can you, the professional, be in control of a transaction, especially if the client's knowledge exceeds yours?

Be gracious. Always compliment the client. Listen. Appeal to the client's ego. You are invaluable through your technical skills and service to the client.

How does an agent, in particular an agent new to the travel industry, achieve product knowledge in the least amount of time? The novice agent cannot very well travel around the world to gather first-hand information before assisting others planning a trip.

But, product knowledge can be instant. The catch is you must be as smart as Karen. It didn't take Karen long to discover which were the most popular destinations in her market area of Lubbock, Texas - trips to Hawaii and cruises to the Caribbean!

In one day, Karen became a very well-versed expert on both of these destinations. She called the marketing departments of the best tour operators in those two markets and asked to be informed about their product. She taped the conversations and later on her way home from the office, she repeatedly listened to the recorded information.

The next day, she felt secure, confident and enthusiastic. She sold nothing but Hawaii and Caribbean cruises. Clients approaching Karen about other destinations ended up going to Hawaii or on a Caribbean

Cruise. Why not? Karen's presentations were simply irresistible and she had discovered some very special offers.

An excellent source for product knowledge are our products themselves: the brochures. They are full of exciting information that researchers have conscientiously put together for the consumer. Unfortunately, many consumers do not enjoy reading. They want to be told what is printed inside the brochure.

So, why not study a brochure each day? Pretend you are going on a trip yourself. You might really get involved in the product then. Each new season, I make it a point to familiarize myself with the new brochures featuring the products I prefer to sell. I use postcards - most of which I obtained on trips or from various tourist offices - as sales tools to help create the picture of the places I try to bring alive. The chance to close a sale rises and falls with the quality of a presentation.

An additional source for product knowledge are sales representatives from the different tour and cruise lines. When these representatives call on our office, we invite them to make a presentation. Sometimes we record the presentation and examine it later.

Sales Tips, here are a few pointers on making the best sale possible:

*   Remember the importance of your expression. Clients do not want to deal with an unpleasant travel counselor.
*   Be prepared to ask the right questions. The questions you ask may enhance the pleasures of the trip and also help prevent a disastrous trip.
*   Get the client involved. The client should not feel as if he is taking a trip you want to take instead of one he wants to take.
*   Advise the client of any specials that may be in effect, allowing increased mileage for special programs such as upgrading from one class to another, free hotel rooms, free airline tickets, free rental cars and other benefits.
*   Lead the conversation in an elegant and informative, yet fun manner. By treating others as ladies and gentlemen, we emerge as ladies and gentlemen ourselves. And, remember, your goal is to be likable.

* Make it your routine to always rise from your chair to demonstrate that you are delighted to work with each client.
* Hand the client your business card.
* Smile. Smile. Smile.
* Be in control, but always remain polite.
* Be enthusiastic and remember: The trip takes place right at your desk!

# CHAPTER 7

# STARTING

*"Dress for the job you want, not for the job you have"* –Anonymous

Financial security. Luxurious office furniture. A secretary. More free time. Social success. These are the dreams one often envisions when starting a new business. While these things are helpful, they are not necessary. They do not form a reliable foundation on which to build a lasting enterprise.

A high amount of energy and personal values of leadership are far more important. I began my travel agency business with a lean budget, a two-room office, homemade decorations and furniture and just me to perform most of the tasks. But, I have what it takes to succeed in business:

I am blessed with a never-ending supply of energy and the devotion and passion for my job that most people have only for their hobbies and recreational activities. And, I have a loyalty to my own personal style that helps me survive the most difficult of situations.

The Making of a Success

What made Picasso a maestro of paintings? Shakespeare a successful writer? Beethoven a lasting composer? Each genius developed their own, personal style. Each devoted more time than any of their contemporaries to what, at first, was not more than a hobby. And, they each enjoyed their hobby with the passion of an addict.

There is no substitute for commitment, enthusiasm and passion - not even money. Giants like Henry Ford, Aristotle Onassis and, in the travel industry, Arthur Tauck all started their empire without great fortune. But, each kindled an excitement about the product they were willing to devote their time and energy to.

## Financing the Business Venture

When my husband D.C. accepted the position of associate dean of the Graduate School at Texas Tech in Lubbock, time was right for me to open my travel agency - Envoye Travel. When I began planning to open my own business, I suppose I could have borrowed the money and started in grand style. But, I was still very much tied to my German custom of doing only what you can afford to pay for in cash.

My earnings from working as a travel agent at Braley Travel combined with my husband's salary at Texas A&M had allowed us to buy a small farm on the Brazos River about 10 miles south of College Station. Now, our investment and conservative lifestyle paid off as we were able to use the farm as collateral to start our own agency.

I realized that to start a business with borrowed money means that you do not actually own the business. Your actions are restricted by the interest of the true owner - either the bank or the person who invested the money in your business.

Today, of course, I know that if I had borrowed the money, I would not have all these wonderful memories of struggling to make it in the travel business. Also, I would not have the sense of pride which comes with knowing that what counts in life is the distance you have walked between "have not" and "have."

## Starting Out

In the beginning, I filled all the positions in my new company. During daylight, I was Sigrid, the travel counselor. At night, I wore the hats of bookkeeper, planner, and ticket delivery person. On Sundays, I became the carpenter, decorator, cleaning woman, advertising executive, and paper worm.

Through the years, I've encountered a variety of interesting situations, but the worst scenario occurred when I still delivered all the tickets to the customers myself. I chose to perform this particular service at night for two reasons:

a)   The phones in the office didn't stop ringing until the sun had set; and

b)   Nobody would recognize me at night.

The latter was of great importance to me because I was not only Sigrid, the travel agent, I was also Mrs. D.C. Carter, wife of a distinguished university professor, and I did not wish to be seen delivering tickets to all of his colleagues.

I felt I owed it to D.C. to refrain from stooping so low as to deliver airline tickets. Typical German logic, I suppose. One evening as I delivered tickets, I was caught in the act by one of D.C.'s university colleagues. Here is how it happened:

It was after midnight as I drove up to the corner where Dr. Albert Ellis lived in an elegant area of town. I purposely parked my car on the corner, away from Dr. Ellis' house to make sure he would not hear the noisy engine of my old car. As I tiptoed across the brick walkway through the front yard toward the house, carefully looking around like a burglar, I did not realize Dr. Ellis owned a German shepherd who guarded the house like it was Fort Knox.

As I reached to drop the airline ticket in the door slot, the dog started to bark fiercely from inside the house. Immediately, all the lights in the house went on and the windows lit up like something in a Radio City Christmas Spectacular. I saw Dr. Ellis' shadow inside the house march toward the front door. He was holding something in his hand. As fast as I could, I ran toward the nearest tree and hoisted myself up into the top branches.

I did not realize dogs have such an enormous instinct for smelling things. As soon as Dr. Ellis opened the front door, the German shepherd rushed out of the house and toward my tree. His fur standing straight on his back and his skin around his snout pulled up in wrinkles, he barked up my tree.

I was petrified. Dr. Ellis walked toward the tree. "Ah-ha!" he shouted as he pointed the bright flashlight in his hand right into my face. "You? Why, if it isn't D.C's wife. What are you doing up there in the tree?" he asked, genuinely surprised.

"Delivering your airline tickets," I said with a smile, waving the Delta Airlines ticket jacket in my hand.

## Overcome Impossible Handicaps

Indeed, I enjoy the challenge of trying to overcome a handicap. There is a great feeling in being able to do what others consider to be impossible.

When we first started our business, we lacked money for office expenses. I convinced my husband that it was foolish to spend our money on expensive office furniture and that I could build chairs, desks, benches and shelves, and that I could decorate the office with the souvenirs I had collected from my travels. Having to improvise not only stretches your imagination, it often makes for fond memories.

Take my first executive chair, which, of course, I built myself. I constructed it out of wooden two-by-fours left over from a wall we had cut out to connect two offices (I can never throw anything away.) The finished chair was not all that bad. It wasn't quite as sturdy as I had anticipated, but since I only weighed 108 pounds, I figured it would suffice.

It was not a masterpiece, but it fit in with the rest of my New Guinea decor quite well. Stepping back away from the chair and admiring it from distance, I got a proud, warm feeling in my heart. Nevertheless, I was glad that my new "throne" was obstructed from public viewing by my desk.

One day, a very ritzy lady came to my office to ask about organizing a trip to England to study water coloring for the Junior League. Politely - excited at seeing a potential for big business - I ushered her to my desk. After she took a seat, I sat down, carefully, on my new executive chair.

I had never heard of the Junior League. I instantly thought of Little League baseball and could not quite grasp the idea of junior league baseball players wanting to travel all the way to England to brush watercolors on delicate canvas. Therefore, I opened our conversation with a question:

"Of course I am interested in organizing a trip for your group, but, in order to do the best job, I would like to ask, do your little fellows play baseball or football?"

The woman just looked at me somewhat indignantly with a baffled expression. She quickly explained the woman's organization to me.

"The Junior League is a club for ladies under age 40 with the financial stature of limiting needs in our society," she said.

She seemed pleased about having enriched my knowledge in life, and I continued to be excited over the prospect of new business - so excited that I forgot the delicate construction of my chair.

Suddenly, the chair beneath me gave away, and, slowly, one two-by-four collapsed. Too embarrassed to let on what was happening, I held on for dear life with both hands and arms to the desk top, pretending to be seated. From her side of the desk, my customer could not see the chair had sagged. For all she knew, I was still seated. I remember thinking, "Dear God, please let this lady depart soon, and for heaven's sake do not let the phone ring." If I had to reach for the phone, I would most likely fall and I knew it would be impolite to rise from my seat before my client did.

Of course, as luck would have it, the phone did ring. Fortunately, someone else answered it. And, I did get the ladies' business! I sent several members of the Junior League on an adventure to England to take watercolor lessons from a British artist.

Shortly before the group departed for England, I asked the woman why she chose to book her trip with my travel agency. I knew there was another travel agent in town whose owner not only was a member of the Junior League but also managed an office far more elegant than mine.

She replied that she chose me because I was so pleasant to work with and they felt that I knew what I was talking about. She said she felt so at ease asking me any question that popped into her mind. She said I never gave her the feeling that she was inconveniencing me. Not a bad impression considering my office furniture was constructed with souvenirs and two-by-fours!

Do It for The Right Reasons

Based on these and many other experiences, I advise all travel counselors who are swept by the desire to own their own travel agency: Examine all of your options, and ask yourself, "Why do I want to own my personal travel agency?" If the answer involves the desire for more personal freedom, more money, more spare time, I advise you to reconsider.

Do It For the Love of the Industry

Before opening your own travel agency ask yourself, "Do I love the travel industry with enough passion to become a maestro at it? Would I enjoy spending most of each day at it like a favorite hobby? Or, do I want to start my own business to make a bundle of money?"

If money is the answer, it is a dangerously wrong reason. Remember, money should be looked at only as a fringe benefit to your uncompromising devotion to your job. But, even if you should make a lot of money, more important than the money is the fulfillment and satisfaction you gain from performing a job you love.

I have learned, that in any successful business venture, the joy of performing must come first. Only then will money flow in your direction.

Forget Free Time

Maybe you want to start your own business to be boss and have more free time? Wrong again. The future business owner who believes he or she will have more free time once he or she is the boss will soon discover that time spend away from the shop results in losses of earnings.

It is just like when he or she was an employee and missed work and did not get paid for it. However, the losses which occur during the boss's personal absence are much higher.

Being the Boss Means More Responsibility

Maybe you want to start your own business so you can be the boss and do whatever you fancy? Wrong again! To be your own boss does not eliminate obligations. On the contrary, the boss has a tighter time schedule to follow and more obligations to keep than any employee.

Would You Really Be the Boss?

When considering a new venture, many prospective businesspersons make their plans based on the assumption that someone else will provide the financial backing for their businesses. But, remember, you are only your own boss if you start the business with your own money. If you start it with someone else's money, you have the investor's expectations to live up to.

Another danger of starting your business with borrowed money is the percentage of earnings that will actually be yours. The travel industry pays an average of about 10% on airline ticket sales and not much more on tour or cruise sales, especially to the beginner. Your investor might expect a return on his investment that is close to your earnings.

One aspect to examine when considering borrowing money is the ethics and morals of the lender. Your obligation to the lender must be within the framework of your personal morals and honor.

Every shopping center makes it tempting to lease a new location. Furniture stores make it attractive to purchase the latest fine office "necessities." Nobody ever has any problem spending money. But, only a few make money, and even fewer hold on to the money they make.

How often do you hear the popular phrase, "You have to spend money in order to make money"? What nonsense!

It most certainly is not my style. It does not even inspire or excite me. On the contrary, I get an enormous satisfaction out of creating something out of nothing. To turn a pile of compost into a bed of lilies is my style. It is the ultimate achievement!

To create things out of nothing increases the sense of accomplishment. It demands nothing less than a dream so powerful that it wakes you up at night. It also requires a burning desire, commitment, and a sprinkling of sweat.

You Must Have Staying Power

Once you have decided to go into business for yourself, the hard part starts.

My mother used to tell me, "It's easy to get married, strike a new friendship, start a new job or a new business. It's easy to start most anything. What is difficult, is to stay, and to succeed."

To succeed in marriage, keep a friendship, maintain a job, or stay in business, that's what really counts! Yes, as I learned, Mother was right. It is so much easier to start a new business, than to remain in business.

For your "hobby" to become a success, it takes the same amount of passion, long hours, testing, trying, and devotion that it took Michelangelo to carve a sculpture or paint a masterpiece. For you to become a maestro in your field, it takes a Beethoven's amount of patience for hanging in there and endless hours of practice.

## It Takes A Never-ending Devotion

I like to think that all of the positive attributes I encourage others to develop are part of my style. Whether it is true or not, I don't know, but I like to think it is. I am devoted to all aspects of travel. I love the travel industry. It is my hobby: not only the physical act of traveling, but even the technicalities, down to working out the smallest details in a client's travel plans. It's all my hobby.

This passion and love for the travel industry was why I started my business! When I first started my business, I regretted that there were not enough hours in the day to do what I enjoyed. Testing out flight schedules, prices, other travel options, building itineraries, creating plans for incentive travel - it was, and still is, all a fascinating art.

When working late at night, all alone in my office, I would work undisturbed as the whole world slept. I would work until the little door on my cuckoo clock would pop open and the small bird inside would shout "Geh' heim, Geh' heim (go home, go home)" twelve times, reminding me that it was later than I thought - long past my competitors' bedtime.

## Personal Honor - My Way

I am a bit hesitant to tell you about part of what is my style - my version of personal honor. It concerns something my caring friends warned me about when I went into business. And, in a way, they were right.

When I told my friends about opening my own agency, they laughed and said, "Sigrid, you're a romanticist. You are not a businesswoman. In order to be a success in business, you have to be tough. Tough to the extent of being shrewd. You must bow to the power of the dollar and compromise your honesty and your idealistic sense of honor."

Of course, I had never planned to be a businessperson to begin with. It just happened. I emerged a businessperson because I discovered an industry I fell in love with and enjoyed devoting all my energy to. It was all a very natural process.

However, I have succeeded in business and in keeping intact my set of values. And, today, keeping those values and my personality alive is still one of my biggest priorities.

Recently my faithfulness to my values and personal honor were tested. Ronald Shilling, a super salesman, approached me and said, "You need a home computer."

"Why?" I asked. "Because you are going to love it," he said.

"Oh, yeah," I thought, "husband, dogs, cats, fish, ducks, 4,000 wild Canadian geese on the lake that I toss corn to every morning, a computer at home is just what I need." But, maybe he was right. I loved everything I had at home. Problem was, I just never was home very much.

Then I thought, since Shilling was one of my clients why not let him make a little commission and buy the computer.

The test of my values came when it was time to pay for it. Who was going to pay for the computer? The office or I personally?

"It's an office expense, totally tax deductible," Shilling said smiling. He had never heard such a silly unbusinesslike question. Everybody he ever knew claimed everything possible as a business expense.

I decided to call my husband and ask him what he thought. He told me it depended on how much time I would use it for office work and how much time it would be used for personal use. I explained I did not quite know for sure how much was business and asked what I should do.

He said, "When in doubt, follow your style." I did. I pulled out my personal check and handed it to Shilling.

"Here," I said. "Honor buys you more pleasures than money." I thought to myself, "If every U.S. citizen would be as unselfish and honest as my husband, we would not have a national debt. He is the only person I know who voluntarily is paying more income tax then required by law. There are many deductions we could claim, but we don't."

After the decision to buy the home computer with my personal money, I felt an inner strength and pride.


Be Yourself

In short, my style consists of a joy for my job as if it were my favorite hobby, not spending money I do not have, and placing personal honor before monetary benefits. I have always had my way of doing things, regardless of my friends' attitudes. Compromising my values is no more a part of my style than is changing my appearance to fit someone else's image of a successful businesswoman.

Female executives of the early sixties, transformed their hairstyle into a teased, stiff beehive sculpture and wore a lot of makeup. Not me, I wore no make-up, and kept my hair the way my husband liked it best - long, unteased and unsprayed.

"Now that you're a career woman you have to look like one and cut your hair," my good friend Karola said. I didn't respond to her comments.

My thought was, "Karola, I shall prove to you that I can be a success even though I am not going to adopt the present beehive fad." I was not going to spend all that time each morning to look different than what I really was. I would much rather invest the time needed for putting on a disguise into product research and travel. I will keep my hair natural and be myself.


Look for Life's Advantages - Not The Disadvantages

I was always stubborn. In looking back at my childhood school days in Germany, I realize I never was one to succumb to peer pressure.

"Exposures to peer pressure are a marvelous opportunity to test and to practice your leadership skills. At best, it will teach you to be a leader, and, at worst, it will prove you weak," my mother would say. It made sense to me! My mother was a very wise woman, and she was right. For some reason, I always emerged as a leader among my friends.

Shortly after my debut as a business owner, a female reporter from the local newspaper, the Lubbock Avalanche- Journal, appeared in my office, asking me for an interview. I was flattered and accepted. The woman suggested, "I know you must have many disadvantages being a woman in the business world."

Laughing, I replied, "No. Frankly speaking, I never really thought about it. I'm too occupied with the daily pressing issues. But now that you've asked, I realize that being a woman in the business world actually offers a great many advantages."

"How?" the reporter asked. "Take a business meeting for instance," I said. "We women always have the chance to speak first - tradition, I suppose. The poor men have to be polite and wait until we decide we have nothing left to say!"

## Find the Advantages in the Disadvantages

Although I try to find advantages rather than disadvantages, life's little disadvantages sometimes find me. Fortunately, at an early age, I learned to try and turn any possible disadvantage into an advantage. Surviving is a fringe benefit of poverty, I suppose. Complaints and excuses are a waste of time and not for me. I buried my crutches a long time ago.

I never saw the problems my friends saw. I found most problems in life were worked out best by just taking action on them. All it took was personal energy. I guess I have always been lured by challenges. The more impossible a situation the more fascinated and determined I was to go for it!

Yesterday I penned a new sign for the wall of our office restroom that reflects this philosophy. The small yellow note reads: "What I like most about success, is that it does not come easy."

## Testing the Waters

For those who are interested in opening their own travel agency but still have some reservations, I recommend that they first test the waters as an outside salesperson, a position which will allow you the greatest possible freedom of the travel industry.

As an outside salesperson, you are only responsible for your own actions. You can work whatever hours you wish, and you can work them at the office or from your home. You can recruit your own clients.

Outside salespersons arrive at a commission sharing scale with the company they represent. Bear in mind that if you receive half of the commission generated by the sale, you have a more than fair situation because the other half retained by your company is not profit, but is your contribution toward the cost of operation of the company.

## A Plan to Follow

For travel counselors who entertain the wish of ownership, I recommend the following plan:

First, ask your superior if you can work in the bookkeeping department for a while. That should give you an idea of operational costs of an agency. If your desire to open your own agency survives that experience, then you are wise to practice your talents in two other important areas: recruiting customers and meeting monthly financial obligations.

The best way to learn the reality about these two important aspects of the business is test your skills. Ask your supervisor to work out a situation in which you can keep all your commission and then turn around and pay your prorated share of the office rent, advertising, telephone costs, bookkeeping expenses, ticket delivery service, and all general costs which occur to the company during each month. You should also be expected to pay an administrative fee that is reasonable to both you and the building owner.

The result of such an arrangement is a true-to-life experience of what it is like to be a business owner. This realistic perspective will raise your awareness of the obligation a business owner faces each month, and it will introduce you to the responsibilities of managing a successful business.

By all means, resist the temptation of starting at the top of a business. Start at the bottom. Become thoroughly familiar with the roots of the business before investing any capital in an enterprise not completely familiar to you.

One has a greater chance of succeeding if one has a thorough understanding of all aspects of the venture.

## Watch for Hidden Opportunities

The first time I ever got the idea of opening a travel school was when one of the businessmen from a neighboring office came to me and asked if I would train his nephew to be a travel agent.

He said he had watched me run my business and felt his nephew would learn more about business from me than any business school or university. And, besides, he was willing to pay me well!

I remember thinking, "This is the third such request. There was the man on the 5th floor who wanted me to train his son and another on the 9th floor also. I could actually earn money by opening a school."

As you guessed, I saw the opportunity and seized it. Today, I still own and operate a travel agency school out of one of my branch offices.

In Retrospect

A colleague recently asked me, "Would you do it again? Would you again open your own travel agency" Of course I would - because I enjoy challenges!

The more difficult the challenge, the greater my joy. There is nothing in my personal history that I would like to erase or change, including going through the war in Germany, which at times was extremely hard.

All the experiences of my past made me what I am today.

And, today is too magnificent to risk with wishes for changes in the past! Looking into my past, I am just as grateful for the obstacles along my path as I am for the open doors. It's those obstacles which gave me the chance to find out things about myself I might not have known otherwise. They gave me a chance to prove myself and to practice my attitude, my patience, my tolerance, my tastes, and my judgment of other people's situations.

The more versatile the experiences in a person's life, the more complex the person and the more colorful a life they live. Therefore, yes, I would do it all over again - I would open my own business! Your experiences may not be the same as mine, but they have made you the kind of person who would buy this book - the kind of person who would dare to dream, who would learn a new job, and who would welcome the challenges and the privileges of being a travel agency owner!

# CHAPTER 8

# INNOVATION AND CONTROL

*"Don't find fault, find a remedy."*—Henry Ford

When I launched my travel service in 1971 in Lubbock, Texas, several other agencies in the city were already well established. A few years later, the agencies which had preceded mine had vanished. Consequently, Envoye Travel, my agency, is now the oldest travel service in Lubbock.

What did I do right? What did I do differently from my competitors? One of the things I did right was that I had the best cheering section rooting me on! When business looked tough, people cheered me on by assuring me that I had a great positive attitude and more perseverance than anybody they knew! When innovation and energy were at stake, they told me, I would rise above the norm!

If you do not have your own personal cheering section, YOU can be your own best fan! And, don't forget that I am here to help cheer you on, too!

If you follow my advice, you will soon have your own cheering section full of people. First, there will be your travel agency owner who appreciates your hard work, your enthusiasm, and your dedication. Later, there will be your employees who admire your fairness, your encouragement, and your example as you work beside them!

My Secrets: What I Do Differently From My Competitors

Throughout this book, I share with you my secrets for success. And, here are some more secrets that have set me and my travel agency apart from my competitors which, if you follow them, will give you the success you seek!

You can always learn - if you are open to it! As a new travel agency owner, I attended a local meeting among my colleagues. I felt like the new kid on the block and didn't say much.

But, what blew my mind were all the problems my peers were groaning about - travel industry problems I had never even thought about. The problems and objections my colleagues raised sounded reasonable, and the agents attending the meeting seemed intelligent.

I wondered, "Why have I never detected these problems? Maybe I am missing out on something? Maybe I do not have my facts straight?"

After studying the situation, I discovered that it was not that I did not encounter the same problems, but that I had a different way of approaching and dealing with various situations. I thoroughly enjoy my job, and if someone enjoys what they are doing, one eventually will be a success at it! You will find this is true, too.

Much of my success stems from the fact that I represent the interests of my clients with the same passion as I pursue my own interests. I treat my staff with respect and as friends, and I give them all the freedom they ask for. My success continues because I enjoy the changes in our industry and I always look for the new opportunities that come with change. I also do what it takes to keep up enthusiasm and energy levels, and I am constantly trying to further my knowledge of travel products.

The secrets of my success come from all directions!

I am not afraid to make a fool of myself. After all, what would the world be like if we cannot laugh about ourselves once in a while? I approach every project with the intention of giving it everything I have, trying at all times to do the best job possible.

The sensation of the early success of my firm was like a recognition that challenged me to work even harder. I worked longer hours and took greater risks, but I never went out on a limb financially.

I watched our firm's expenses like a hawk. I knew only the government could print money and make it legal!


Experience Attracts Customers

Even in the beginning, clients repeatedly told me how much they enjoyed talking travel with me and how much they appreciated all my suggestions and my knowledge. They assured me that I was the best travel agent they knew and frequently recommended me to their friends.

One thing that I had going for me was that I actually could claim that I had been to most countries in the world. There were several countries where I had lived and, by doing so, had become a part of their cultures.

Remember, if you haven't been to all these places yet, you can go there by reading and researching the places in the brochures and by talking to representatives of the firms in the brochures. The trip takes place at your desk - until you have the opportunity to travel yourself! And, that opportunity to travel, like a millionaire, will come sooner than you think!

As you gain more experience from your own travels, you can use these experiences as I have. Not only were the experiences invaluable in helping clients plan their trips, but I decorated my office walls with souvenirs and newspaper clippings showing me in different parts of the world. One picture showed me at the palace in Lima as guest of the president of Peru, and in another I was with the famous mud men in New Guinea.

As travel agent, I continue traveling. However, I learn much more on travel agency familiarization trips than the average travel agent does because I frequently can speak to the locals in their own language. Speaking a foreign language opens foreign doors and foreign friendships.

I also become intimate with a particular location by moving around much faster than the average person. This makes it possible for me to inspect twice as many hotels, research more facilities, and visit more tourist attractions than do many of my peers.

Frequently on trips, my peers cling together. They party and have a good time, however, I feel I can do that at home. When I am abroad, I want to learn as much as I can.

I sneak away from the group. To investigate a place all alone is my favorite way to explore. It intensifies my experiences.

Office Finances

Every Tuesday, when the financial department settles our debts to the airlines, a computer printout is posted on the office bulletin board. So, on

Tuesdays, every counselor is very eager to see the amount of commission he or she generated.

One-third of the commission generated by each agent goes back to the agent. The agent who generates the highest amount of commission during one month wins a special bonus check.

Agents have a chance to be paid a salary rather than a commission, but 99 percent of my agents prefer the commission system. The salaried agents are paid according to the average level of their production.

In a way, each counselor at Envoye South determines his or her income. D.C. and I, the legal owners, use the profit which remains after the agents are paid to finance the running of the business. We retain a reasonable amount as a return on our investment and risk-taking.

What is left is distributed at the end of the year in the form of extra bonuses to the agents and in donations to a social cause. For example, last year we gave a check to the Rotarians for the purchase of a special machine designed to help a disabled child in Lubbock!

Quite by accident, I found out that the fact that we give a percentage of our profit to a social cause adds to the incentive for higher sales among several of my agents. As I casually mentioned our donation to Mari Ann, her response was that it really made her feel good because, in a way, the donation included her efforts as well.

I am quite certain that it is far more inspiring for a staff member to see their efforts benefit a noble cause than to have the owner live in a mansion or drive a deluxe car.

The fact that we channel some of our firm's profit into social causes has added extra meaning to my job. It has motivated me to work twice as hard. Judging by Mari Ann's remark, I am certain my enthusiasm for my cause has spilled over into the hearts of some of my co-workers as well.

During the Persian Gulf War, I decided to work one hour longer every day as part of my way of supporting our service people over there. The extra hour should result in extra profits which will result in extra taxes that will support our country's goal in the war.

It is only one of the things I do to support our people serving over there so far away from home. And, it may not seem like such a large contribution by itself, but think what a tremendous help it would be to them and to our government if we were all working longer and paying more taxes.

Advertising

Advertising has joined the list of the other joint responsibilities in our Envoye South office (Continue on to Chapter 10, Leadership in the Office, for more details on joint responsibilities in an office).

During the week, counselors keep their eyes open for special vacation packages. Their final selections will be advertised. In our area, newspaper advertising has a higher success rate than radio or television advertising. When we choose television as our medium, we select a product which is featured during the show.

For example, during the time the show The Love Boat enjoyed popularity on television, we regularly ran a cruise ad during the commercial break. The cruise line paid half of the expenses for the ad through a practice called cooperative advertising.

My company has benefitted enormously through free advertising. I have written weekly travel essays for a Lubbock newspaper, the Lubbock Times, and a senior citizens' paper. In return, the newspapers run my ads free of charge.

KFYO, a local radio station, invited me to host a travel show every Wednesday morning. I paid for my company ad during the show, which was of a very minor cost while the benefits were enormous. The show did not necessarily sell a particular travel product, but it introduced me personally to the public as the travel agent they should contact when travel was on their minds. It made my name synonymous with travel.

Every Wednesday, I took the listener on another portion of my one-year adventure of hiking through South America. There is no way of placing a monetary value on the sales that resulted from the radio show because the success still continues.

Even today, 10 years later, hardly a month goes by without someone coming to my office and saying, "Sigrid, I remember you from way back when you talked about your canoe trip through the Amazon on the radio." The radio travel show gave me an image in my community that of immeasurable value.

In almost everything I do, "travel" is with me and plays an important part. When I was asked to open my house for a fund raiser during the Christmas season, I couldn't help but seize the opportunity of injecting "travel" into the project.

Several of my counselors offered to decorate a Christmas trees in the tradition of their native countries. Shini decorated a Korean Christmas tree; Rita, one from Germany, Peter, one from Yugoslavia. And, the newspaper covered the event while our agency established itself as being manned by experts in foreign countries!

Every opportunity I have, I give travel talks. I offer my topic to organizations, schools, and churches. I communicate to the audience that travel really is affordable to anyone. I tell them that in Germany the people budget the cost of their vacation into their monthly budget.

All a person has to do is forego buying a soft drink and a candy bar each day. Put aside as little as one dollar a day. At the end of the year, voila! The person has saved $365. And, at the present time, $365 will allow a traveler to stay one week at the Hotel Playa de Oro in Puerto Vallarta, flying round-trip from Lubbock, Texas.

Of course, there is always the opportunity to organize a trip for a group and for the individual who takes on the responsibility to earn a free trip (See the Chapter 16, Other Ways to Travel Like a Millionaire: Increasing Outside Sales, for more details on free trips available when someone organizes a group).

When making a presentation, I have an objective in mind: I want the audience to remember me and the name of my company. That way, when the need for a travel agent arises, they will think of me.

To create a visual picture in the spectators' minds - known to be one of the most effective memory devices - I connect my name to a story. For instance, I mention to the audience how relieved I was when I finally did not have to spell my name for clients calling into the office - all because we had a new president with a name just like mine: Carter!

After the presidential election, when the first caller inquired about vacation arrangements and asked me to spell my name, I happily replied, "My name is Carter - just like the new president!"

"Oh," the caller said, "Corder?"

The Yellow Pages

At the time, I thought it was the worst business decision I have ever made - purchasing the half-page ad in the telephone book's Yellow Pages.

When I signed the contract, I was 100 percent certain that the high price was for the entire year. However, a month later, I discovered the high price I had reluctantly agreed to was per month. Never in a million years would I have agreed to spend that much money on an advertisement! So, what happened?

It was a gold mine! I discovered a gold mine, and all because of a mistake.

I had no idea that the first thing Americans do when they need something - anything - is to look in the refrigerator. If they can't find it there, they look in the Yellow Pages.

That was nearly twenty years ago. I have renewed the ad each year, and this year I even went to a full-page ad. My only complaint is that I wish the telephone company wouldn't list Travel right after Trash!


Dealing with Office Problems

No matter how well-run an office is, from time to time difficulties will arise. There are many ways of dealing with the problems that can pop up. Solutions are always there for those of us who have a desire and the imagination to look for them! Here are some general tips to follow when you're confronted with a problem in the office.

In our office, problems are addressed no sooner than 24 hours after they occur. Within 24 hours, the intellect usually wins the upper hand and a great majority of the problems have faded away and are no longer an issue.

Time tends to settle the high tide of human emotions. D.C. taught me never to talk negatively or discuss a problem after 6 p.m. when the mind and the body need to regenerate for the following day. Some problems involve only one person and require a bit of diplomacy.

Nobody could have worked harder than Gretchen, but Gretchen's sales were poor. I knew the reason why, but my instinct warned me, that if I criticized Gretchen, things might turn from poor to disastrous. Gretchen's sales-killer was her whiney tone of voice. It was as uninspiring as lukewarm water. What she had to say was great, but the way she said it was worthless.

Her voice lacked any power of conviction. She sounded skeptical whenever she said even the most wonderful things. I decided to make a general office suggestion. The company would provide a recorder that could be hooked into the telephone system, giving every agent the chance to record their voice and to judge their manner.

"My gosh," Gretchen told me a week after my suggestion. "I had no idea my voice sounds like that of a wimp," she laughed.

We talked about the importance of voices and how tone sends a much stronger message than words. The tone in an agent's voice will make or break a sale. Keep in mind, that you will never regret something you didn't say.

We started a game in the office. Once a month, each staff member could submit one of their own voice recordings to win the first prize for best telephone voice of the month. The entire office staff had fun participating. It wasn't too long until Gretchen won the first prize!


In Times of Crisis

This time it was more than a crisis. It was a complete disaster! Our downtown office experienced a major theft. Someone I trusted embezzled money from the company.

At the time, I was capable of only one sentiment: How could my company survive? But, survive it would. I was determined to keep my company in business. I had to act fast, and borrowing money was not my style, self-reliance was. Any dollar I did not have, I could compensate with my energy.

With the majority of my company's money gone, I had to find a fast source of additional income. What followed confirmed my belief that from adversity comes creativity.

I never told anybody this, but that's when I decided to extend the business hours of Envoye Travel South. I chose Envoye South because I was already officed there, and I did not want to infringe on the managers' authority in my other two offices by asking them to change their system and to work longer hours.

When we first offered longer hours, the office suffered from a lack of clients during the late evening. However, I filled the time by offering computer training classes to those interested in joining the travel industry.

Soon afterwards, I realized that these emergency arrangements were going to be a blessing in disguise. The results that came from that theft were astounding.

Being open on Sundays offers the benefit of attracting those travelers who examine the Sunday newspaper's travel section. Since most of these readers work the rest of the week, they appreciate the fact that they do not have to postpone their curiosity. Sunday was also the best time because clients were vacation mood. They are very septic to vacation mood. Envoye South, was the only travel service open on Sundays in Lubbock.

I was amazed at how many calls referred to my competitors' ad. The clients did not care which agency they talked to. All the client was looking for was instant information on Sunday when it is most convenient for them to think of travel. Being open evenings attracts young professionals to get together and visit my office.

We entertain with travel videos, and frequently, clients assure us how much they appreciate us being open during evenings. Daytime is not always a convenient time for them to get together. It conflicts with their jobs. Many evening clients hold responsible positions during the daytime, which allow a budget for travel.

The lessons to be learned? Every problem has a solution! With the right solutions, all problems are turned into winning, and profitable situations!

Convenience: The Benefit Of Expanding Your Operating Hours

How important is it to your business to be open evenings, holidays, weekends?

One headline says it all: "Albertson's (a food store chain) is recession-proof due to its aggressive hours of operation!"

A travel agency should be no exception. We want to be recession-proof as well, don't we? A client might not necessarily trade "after regular business hours," but the fact that the client can, in case of an emergency, is a great advantage for a business to have.

Convenience is important. It is a sample of the kind of service you are willing to give. Convenience is a great indication to your customers that your company really cares about providing them with extraordinary service.

So, it only makes sense that the consumer who is looking for a service-minded travel agent will select the agency with longer, more convenient hours of operation over an agency that is closed when he or she gets off work and is ready to conduct business.

Benefits of Running a Travel School

In addition to being another source of revenue for the business, my travel agency training program has proven to be the perfect source for screening new employees. Ninety percent of the people working at Envoye South now are students from my school.

It was through my school that I also met Jutta. Jutta approached asking me for a nighttime bookkeeper position. She had three children at home she wished to be with during daytime.

Never turning down a new idea until I tried it, I was ready to give this one a chance: a nighttime bookkeeper. So, Jutta worked from 3 a.m. to 7:30 a.m., and during those hours of uninterrupted time, she accomplished the job of two daytime bookkeepers.

It is important for us to understand that it is dangerous for those of us in sales to refer to the customer as "my client" or "our clients." The client will trade where he or she wants to. Even a long friendship will not interfere with that choice. Remember, the client takes his or her business where he or she gets the best service!

A word of caution: By the same token, it is customary for a business owner to use the phrase "my staff."

My staff? Well, there really is not such a thing because we don't own a person. A person is free. Everyone works for him- or herself. My staff is the staff who will punish a company through revenge if mistreated. My staff will decide to work less or purposely cause a mistake just to get even.

I may sometime use the term "my" when referring to "my" employees, but I never forget that these are free people. And, part of my job is to not let them forget their freedom either!

It is important for management to make the employee realize that he or she does not belong to anyone, but they work for themselves. The employee receives a company paycheck. He or she is a free person, and his or her actions reflect not only on the prosperity of the business but also on his or her personal income.

Accessibility

A travel agency owner or manager must be easily accessible to both customers and staff. An owner or manager should not be isolated in a suite away from the action.

I selected the front desk at Envoye South as my roost. Why? Because I want to be where all the action is - right in the front line!

I want to be where I can talk to all the clients who visit our office. I want to see if my firm's clients smile as they depart the office or if they look dissatisfied or indifferent. I have, on rare occasions, detected an indifference in a departing client, and I was able to rescue the situation by suppling additional travel information.

The important part is that my staff knows I am sitting there. It's an efficient way of exercising quality control.

Privacy at Work

Every counselor at Envoye works in a small, yet individual office. The focus is on privacy. I adopted the importance of privacy after my uncle in Germany reinforced the idea that most people work better in privacy. He resigned from his job of 20 years because the bank he worked for was building a new modern office and everyone's desk would be on the same floor without dividing walls for privacy.

Most people need as much privacy as possible in order to perform at an optimum. The private offices protect from any feeling of being observed by management. The feeling of being observed can easily result in intimidation and lead to the employee being preoccupied with pretending to do a job.

Creativity Is the Tool of a Winner

There was the time when I had a request from Jim Johnson, the district governor of the Lubbock Lions Club. He awarded me the business of several dozen members who decided to attend a meeting in Hawaii.

I never tell my clients of any problems, and I always try to keep the enthusiasm for a trip high. I banked on my capability of working out obstacles.

So, I did not tell Jim or anyone else that all airline flights to Hawaii were full. As a last resort, I called the White House and asked to talk to President Gerald Ford.

I didn't talk to the President, but one of his administrators was kind enough to listen to my dilemma. I told the official that all commercial carriers were fully booked, and I had clients willing to pay cash for airline seats to Hawaii.

Wasn't it sensible to make profitable use out of several Air Force planes I had observed sitting idle at Lubbock's Reese Air Force Base?

Didn't the government need the extra money my firm would generate through the additional business?

Could the government afford to lose the revenue it would receive from chartering to me one large transporter plane or several smaller fighter planes?

Wouldn't it be something if the Air Force would start making money by using some of their planes for peaceful use?

These were some of the question I fired at him in my heavy German accent, and then I assured him that I was not going to turn down the use of Air Force One either!

Well, I got a good laugh from the official, but I also got a phone call from a commercial airline a few hours later. I like to think that the reason why the airline called me and suddenly offered me seats for my group, was a direct result of my call to President Ford.

Of, course, I can't be sure, but the important fact was: I had gained another victory. Proof again that once a person's mind is determined to win, the mind will subconsciously make decisions that ultimately lead to success!

It is always the result that counts. Right?

In the end, my clients traveled to Hawaii, and that was the only thing that counted in running a business successfully. The interest of the client always is the ultimate concern.

I make it a point to always reach out for that one more telephone call. It isn't good enough for me to be able to say, "I have tried everything." There are simply too many different possible approaches that can lead to a successful harvest.

Job satisfaction for me comes with the conviction that I have pleased someone and that I have delivered at least one more thing than was expected of me, one more thing than what I promised. That's the moment I am content. That's the moment I enjoy my job the most!

To reach fulfillment in our job isn't always easy. But, fortunately for me, I don't get a thrill out of anything that's too easy.

Have you ever wondered how many "no's" Columbus must have received when he tried to find a sponsor for his wild idea to find a new passage to India? What would have been the consequences had he given up? Nothing much...someone else would have succeeded in his place.


Avoid Getting into Difficulty with a Client

Faultless service is the best remedy to avoid getting into predicament with a client. However, even the most careful agent still can make a terrible mistake. Realizing that all of us make mistakes should at least keep us humble.

If we do make a mistake, we must try everything to correct the mistake. To be defensive about an unpleasant matter and to blame the misfortune on the client makes a bad situation only worse.

There have been times when I knew the client requested a reservation for the same date I issued the airline ticket for. Yet later the client insisted that I had made a mistake in the travel date.

Had I stood my ground, we would have ended up adversaries. Instead, I apologized, assuring the client how sorry I was, and the client's attitude immediately changed.

I avoided anger. In a calm constructive manner, we looked at all the options available to correct the mistake.

Whenever possible, I try to learn from mistakes clients make. I want to learn, to profit, from my mistakes. Adversity can always be an opportunity for the intelligent and dedicated person!

Now, I routinely mention the day of the week in connection with the date. I say "Monday, September 11" instead of just "September 11." It's amazing how this and many other simple safety valves can prevent errors from happening.

The agent who consistently is friendly and helpful and, consequently, well-liked by the client, will never get into turmoil with a client.


Be Smart and Control Business Expansion

In many cases, business expansions are the cause for bankruptcies. Too often business expansions weaken quality control.

To control business expansion, especially during times when business is flourishing, is indeed difficult. Things are going so well. Why stop? Right? Well, during times of success, many business leaders become over-confident and easily fail to realize the limits of quality control.

It is a unique talent for someone who experiences success to be able to suddenly put on the brakes and to decide to resist physical growth in favor of quality growth. It is like walking on the ice of a frozen lake. There comes a point where the ice is too thin to carry that one more daredevil step, but, by then, it is too late.

To resist business expansion might be easier if we realized that business expansion primarily means expansion of obligations and not necessarily higher profits. Profits are a direct result of quality control. I know this to be a fact because I experienced the problems inherent in expansion first hand.

Isn't profit the epitome of business success? A small company can show a bigger profit than a large company does. I learned my lesson on the subject of business growth verses profit growth the hard way. So, several years ago when I was invited to open travel agencies in San Francisco and Chicago, I resisted.

I had already learned a valuable lesson from my fiasco in Midland where I had opened a travel agency. During the time I owned agencies both in Midland and in Lubbock, I found myself losing control over my entire operation. For the first time ever, I began to loath my lifestyle, and I found myself doing things I did not enjoy.

I was driving the 200 miles - the length of one Puccini opera - between Lubbock and Midland several times a month. I was consuming my energy faster than I was able to restore it. I was physically worn out. My mind produced nothing but mediocrity.

The problem? I had spread myself too thin. I had lost control over the quality I wanted my clients to receive.

I finally sold the Midland office. It was a hard choice because, in a way, it spelled failure to close that office. But, I concentrated my efforts on making my agencies in Lubbock the best they could be rather than focusing on the failure in Midland. In looking back, I know I made the right choice.


Experience Helps

Finally, there is one more important factor that enhanced my success in running a business. I brought experience with me when I opened my business.

I brought with me the experience of having been trained by some of the world's foremost service-minded companies, like Deiter in Germany, Vacheron & Constantin in Geneva, Switzerland, Tiffany's in New York, and Gumps in San Francisco.

More importantly, I brought with me the experience of being a servant at the Dr. Mahler Schachter residence in Bromley Kent, England, at Madame and Monsieur Pierre Pellette's home in Lausanne, Switzerland, and for the Trapp family in Stowe, Vermont.

We first must desire to be a success as a servant, to genuinely want to help, if we are going to be successful in sales. We must want to be sensitive toward peoples' needs, to truly want to spoil them.

That is success, and not just success in the business world. That type of personal attitude will brighten our private lives as well.

Playing gauchos in Chile.

# CHAPTER 9

# SAINTS AND SINNERS: WORKING WITH EMPLOYEES

*"No man will make a great leader who wants to do it all himself,
or to get all the credit for doing it."* –Andrew Carnegie

Yesterday two of my best colleagues did not get along. Today they
do. Why? I lied. I told each of them privately how much the other person
liked her.

A firm's greatest asset is its associates. My staff is every bit as
important to me as my clients are. I support them 100 percent. After all,
without my co-workers I wouldn't have very many clients.

In the case of an occasional misunderstanding or confrontation,
my agents know they have my support and together we will face and
hopefully solve a crisis, in a responsible manner.

Recently, when I thanked some of my highly productive and very
loyal people who have been with me for years, they said the reason they
stayed with my firm is because they enjoy the general environment of our
office, the great personal freedom that is so essential in developing self-
confidence, and the fun they have at work.

None mentioned monetary earnings, but I know the highest paid
travel agents in Lubbock are the top producers in my firm. I enjoy people
that seek a high salary, and I respond by telling them what it takes on
their part to achieve that salary.

Why Look at Japan?

In the American business world, we often look at Japan as a model
for good business practice. And, I must confess, I, too, was surprised and

fascinated when I learned that in Japan, a manager voluntarily reduces his salary if the production of his company does not reach the projected profit.

Honor is a great tradition in Japan. Honor is the ultimate success in any person.

Being in awe of the ethics of the Japanese business manager, I compared the honor of the Japanese managers to the honor in my staff. My heart fills with pride when I realize that my managers' honor is every bit as newsworthy as the honor of the Japanese managers.

My company is blessed with leaders that do not need to look to Japan. The example they set is one reason why the United States is still number one in the business world.

Only several weeks ago, one of my managers, Dolores Carpenter, turned down 40 percent of a yearly bonus because Envoye Travel West, which she manages, showed less of a year-end profit than she and I had anticipated.

And, several years ago, when Diane Mitchell first volunteered to move up from the position of travel counselor into the position of manager of Envoye Travel Downtown, she cut the salary I offered her in half, for accepting the managerial responsibilities.

Diane felt my offer was too generous. She did not want to take advantage of me anymore than I wished to take advantage of her.

To keep personal benefits in perspective and at least in line with company earnings is extremely important for company growth. Exploitation will always fail.

Ideally, a firm's owner should put the benefit of the managers first. Likewise, the manager puts the workers first, and the workers put the clients first. If I ever succeed in creating this model company, I would achieve one of my life's highest goals.

To create a company to which every staff member enjoys coming each day, where they feel important and are rewarded a fair share of their production, holds a higher aspiration for me than any amount of money I could draw from my firm's bank account.

It is mind boggling what we learn from situations early in our lives that at first may seem trivial or unfair in our most formative years, but end up being crucial lessons.

In my early life, while living on a farm in Germany, mice ate my only schoolbook. It was irreplaceable. For that, I earned a good whipping from my teacher.

To this youngster, the whipping seemed very unfair. Yet, some twenty years later when I was stranded in the Amazon jungle and surrounded by mice and rats, the whipping jumped back into my memory. I could feel the teacher's bamboo stick strike my fingertips as I was taking every possible precaution so that no rodent could find and chew up my passport. I had to admit that Fraulein Richter's whipping now suddenly came in very, very handy.

Which brings me to another "gone with the wind" incident which seemed unfair to me at the time, but which today benefits me greatly. I was a young woman living in Geneva and working as a sales clerk. My boss spied on my sales performance from behind a curtain. He made me painfully nervous, and I was not able to work well because of it.

Today, that memory and its pain pay their dividends. Now that I am the boss, I will not repeat Monsieur Bergues mistake. I will not intimidate my sales staff in any way.

Instead, I inject my staff with all the confidence possible, because self-confidence is the foundation for any success, and creates a system of awards that has proven most beneficial to all concerned. Self-confidence opens all locks to a person's potential.

Setting the Example

My staff considers me the best sales person in our firm. I know this because most members of my staff, at one time or another, have complimented me on my sales ability. Their kind applause has encouraged me to reach even higher levels of success.

One day, on a long trans-Pacific flight, I had plenty of uninterrupted time to think about my business and staff. I pretended to be asleep so the service-minded flight attendant would stop showering me with tempting chocolates.

I tried to figure out why I was a successful sales person. Then I remembered Monsieur Bergues hiding behind the curtain to spy on me. I decided that the major reason why I was successful was because I did not have to fear criticism. After all, I was the boss, and who would criticize the boss?

Behind closed eyes, as my mind puzzled over how I could contribute to the self-confidence of the members of my staff, I realized that I must give them as much freedom to do their work as I could while still maintaining the control I needed over my business.

I would try to give them as much freedom as I had. And, by giving them the freedom to do their work, I was also letting them know that I had confidence in them.

Back in the office, my first and most important step was to eliminate criticism. When things went wrong, I took a deep breath and looked the other way.

I reasoned that in all likelihood, the mistake bothered the offender as much as it bothered me. I could make a compassionate statement in place of a denouncing one!

My second step was to mainly concentrate on employees' actions that called for praises and compliments. That is harder to do than it sounds since it is human nature to take the good for granted and to jump on the bandwagon of criticism.

At least for a trial period, I was going to reverse my focus and see the glitter only. To my own surprise, I ended up having more fun that way.

Next, I would point out just exactly how easy it was to make a mistake, and I would remind the employee that the number of mistakes a person makes often is closely related to how much a person does.

So, rather than criticizing Charlotte for never stamping any brochures, I put up a sign thanking Wendy and Judie in the name of all of us for stamping brochures. The next day the sign was gone, and Charlotte was stamping brochures.


Inaugurating The Boss's New Attitude

I inaugurated my new attitude by cutting down the distance between myself and my staff. The perfect tool? Show them that I made mistakes, too!

I shared the most humiliating story about myself, the travel "expert," whose knowledge of vacation travel was untouchable. I share it with you now just as I told it to them:

"You will never guess what happened to me several years ago when I had the honor of making travel arrangements for a group of Catholic nuns. The nuns requested a stopover in Paris.

In trying to please them, I was inordinately concerned with keeping their spending at an all-time low. I found this dirt cheap, small hotel on Paris' Left Bank.

When the nuns departed Texas, they were all smiling and full of praises. After all, I had saved them so much money!

When the nuns returned, they laughed telling me about the hotel. I had put them up at a house of ill repute!"

The nuns had a great sense of humor about the mix-up. And, sometimes the clients make the mistakes themselves. In any situation, you will find that a sense of humor is vital to success.

For example, Delores was looking forward to dinner in a Greek restaurant in London. Already, upon entering the casual atmosphere, the laughter coming from the other guests created an inviting environment.

It was going to be a special evening, Delores could tell. And, she knew her husband Randall would appreciate the prices more than he had the previous evening when they had spent a small fortune in one of London's "better-than-France" French restaurants. The menu posted outside indicated that stuffed wine leaves were only 3 pounds sterling - less than $5 in "real money."

"Yes," Delores thought to herself as the maître d' ushered them to a table, "tonight's dinner would make up for the exorbitant cost of last night's meal!"

Stacks of plates were piled on each dinner table. Guests at every table indulged in the Greek tradition of smashing dinner plates on the floor. One by one, ka-bang! Like frisbees, dinner plates were sailing through the air - only to crash and shatter loudly on the ground.

"I bet they charge for these plates!" Randall said as he cautioned Delores not to get carried away.

"Oh, don't be silly! When in Rome, do as the Romans do!" Delores chided. "Here, throw a plate!"

Time came for Randall to settle the dinner bill. Chewing on a toothpick that stuck halfway out of his mouth, he spoke in his slow Texas drawl:

"Last night was a bargain compared to this. I hope you enjoyed it, Honey. You just smashed $150 worth of dinner plates!"

Now, something like that couldn't happen to you. You are too smart for that. You are at least as smart as I am. Right? Great!

So, I call several Mother Superiors. Ask if they and their sisters wish to visit the Pope in Rome. So I fax the Pope a message. Offer him a kickback: x amount of dollars for each nun the Vatican will host. Believe me, it's a very unexplored travel market!

Above all, remember it's all for the fun of it. And, the one who has the most fun, wins!

Just like Schiller said: "Walk your path with joy, like the hero does to victory!" I would humbly add, "Walk your path with joy - the joy which comes from personal freedom!

The Benefits of Personal Freedom on Sales

August is usually the slowest season for a travel agency. Lori and Wendy decided to use this period productively by putting out the seeds for a good harvest down the road.

They started out by compiling a list of accounts they really wanted to have, disregarding the fact that these accounts were already in the hands of competent competitors. As they dropped in "cold" at these businesses, they not only offered their service, but they also brought something with them: appetizing information.

"Did you know you could fly to Hawaii, spend a week, and only pay $620?" was Lori's question to a secretary of one of the accounts she wanted.

Lori's question broke the ice and opened the door to a pleasing conversation. Lori volunteered to include the secretary on her travel agency's mailing list so the secretary would receive the latest information once a month on airfares and convenient schedules to popular destinations.

Before ending her visit, Lori asked "Do you have any trips scheduled right now that I could look at just to see if I could best the price or come up with a better schedule?" When the secretary showed Lori their schedule, Lori was able to point out a few advantages her competitor had overlooked.

As Lori left, she caught the secretary's imagination one last time by advising her not to give one agency a monopoly on all the company's travel:

"The company is bound to get lower airfares and better schedules, if the travel agency knows you are not married to their agency."

If I had to select one trend as the most fundamental for running a successful business with a successful staff, it would be personal freedom - it's what the free market economy is all about!

Yes, allowing each member of your staff the freedom to develop their own potential and to select the personal style of which he or she is most comfortable is very rewarding to all concerned. Anyone can travel like a millionaire provided they are a productive member of the travel industry, whether they are full-time or part-time.

I have already shared with you a few of the magnificent surroundings all over the world in which I have had the privilege of staying. I have even stayed in the Royal Suite in the Imperial Palace Hotel in Vienna and occupied the same splendid room which West Germany's Chancellor Adenauer fancied when he visited the Burgestock Estate near Lucerne, Switzerland. I have trekked the mountains of Nepal with 85 Sherpas looking after my wellbeing and that of the other 11 guests traveling in our party.

Just as I earned these wonderful experiences by creative sales, these experiences are waiting for you and your enthusiastic staff as a reward for making great sales in the travel industry. And, the great sales will come from allowing everyone the personal freedom to do their job in the best way possible!


Office Theft

Office theft is the most serious problem a company faces. It can be a fatal problem, a deadly virus, for any company.

What can be done to prevent in-house theft?

A very successful business person once told me: "Treat everyone like they just jumped bail."

But, I am a trusting person. I enjoy the fringe benefits of trusting others. Trust is so much easier, so much more pleasant to live with, and trust increases office production.

On the flip side of the coin, suspicion devours energy. However, a person's trust provides a great incentive for foul play. My trust in the people on my staff has brought me down to my knees several times during my 20 years as owner of Envoye Travel.

Some of my colleagues believe that an elaborate office control is a safeguard against company theft. However, my experience has taught me that, no matter what controls a company exercises, if someone wants to beat the system, they will find a way.

If thieves only realized the money they could earn if they invested the time it takes to figure out a way to beat the system in being productive in a normal sense. And, I like to think that if these company thieves only realized the heartache they caused, they might not commit the crime.

I shall never forget the disastrous evening when D.C.

came to my office. His face was as white as a sheet, and I knew at once something terrible had happened.

"We are finished," he said. "It's all over." The guilty person was someone we had hired out of pity several years prior to the theft. I taught the person the business and had total confidence in that person. The theft left us with a huge amount of travelers' checks cashed in and gone.

But, we were determined to hang in there.

We opened our office evenings and weekends. We started a travel agent school during the evening hours we were open, and we gave travel programs for various clubs and churches.

The additional business we were able to generate rewarded the extra amount of energy and time we invested. We survived another learning experience!

A colleague of mine in Houston was less fortunate. He lost his business because of a less substantial theft than the one our office experienced. My colleague did not have the energy to stick with it and fight for survival he was so disillusioned with his staff.

Every travel agency manager in town raised their eyebrows when they heard though the grapevine about the clever theft "Lillian" (a fictitious name) inflicted on the agency for which she worked as a travel counselor.

"Lillian" frequently kept clients' cash. When a client paid cash for an airline ticket, "Lillian" just stuffed the cash into her purse. To erase her tracks, she charged the airline ticket on other clients' credit cards.

Lesson learned? The agent responsible for settling the airline ticket sales with the airlines must check and make certain that the name on the airline tickets charged to credit cards is identical to the name on the credit card.

If the names differ, the agent settling the airline account should call the client to verify the form of payment and question the travel counselor who issued the ticket. In our agencies, each counselor is responsible for the payment of each ticket they sell.

I have been fortunate these last few years. No big theft has occurred in any of my three offices.

The main reason might very well be that my staff watches out for would-be thieves. Our system is an imitation of the successful Neighborhood Crime Watch.

Hiring Employees

You can be the best business person possible, but if you do not hire the right people to help you run your business, your business will not survive.

Hiring employees is easy. Anyone can hire somebody. The difficulty is that nobody can actually predict what the new employee will accomplish, until it is too late.

It took me only fifteen years of running a business to discover a secret for hiring the right people. Too bad it took a major office crisis - a substantial theft by an employee - for me to stumble upon a secret for hiring the right office personalities: To recover from the theft, I opened a travel school. I refer to my school as a travel agency training institute!

The more promising students are invited to assist in our office with small tasks to gain practical work experience. The true reason for this is that it will allow me to carefully examine their performance.

In particular, I look for such invaluable talents as public relation skills, the ability to serve, innovation, enthusiasm, communication, and self-motivation. To be self-motivated is a must for people in the travel industry because the experienced, senior agents usually do not have the time to assist newcomers in learning the ropes.

The school gives me total control over testing prospective agents as to their potential of becoming a successful travel agent.

Additionally, when I interview a candidate, I make it an important point to ask how many jobs the applicant has held and what the longest period of employment at any given job was.

How long a person worked for one particular company tells me more about an applicant's general work ethics than the very best resume listing a dozen employers within a few years. It will forecast whether the person is able to work out problems or simply walk away from them.

Furthermore, I will hone in on the applicant's sentiments about his last place of employment. I have learned that often a person's professional success has closer ties to the individual's characteristics than to the place of employment. In most instances, true winners will blossom no matter where they are planted.

I am constantly looking for the winners. But, winners are as rare as winning a lottery ticket.

However, once a year I usually come across a true winner. Since I became a business owner in 1971, I have accumulated quite a few winners.

We established in an earlier chapter that winners in the travel industry rely on the ability to create a visual picture of the destination for the client. If a job candidate has a background in acting or teaching, my attention is caught.

Agents do need to fill orders for tickets and be organized enough to handle the mechanics. But, more importantly, agents need to make the destination come alive for the client while the client is visiting our office. To do this takes a sense of the dramatic and the ability to act out the excitement of a trip, talents for which actors and teachers are trained.

Occasionally I will ask a candidate to describe New England in the fall, a stroll on the Champs' Elysees, or a visit to Westminster Abbey. I will also ask if El Paso is east or west of Dallas and if they know some of the capitals around the world.

To test mechanical talents, I let a candidates fill out a trip cancellation policy, pretending to go on a trip.

My constant search for excellence inspires me to experiment with different hiring methods. Finding people who want to work seems to be the challenge of the future.

In preparation for the new task ahead, during the month of September, I offered everyone a job who asked for one. Maybe it was my good luck that I had only a few takers. And, those who accepted clearly realized the benefit of enrolling in our firm's travel agency training institute.

Sometimes I will let an unknown applicants' efforts during the self-training period be the deciding factor as to whether or not they get a permanent job. Through this particular system, my firm has harvested instant benefits, and I made a marvelous discovery. By giving others a chance, I give myself a chance.

The first thing that I learned, to my great surprise, was that my first impression of others could be lousy. Consequently, some of the people I would never have taken on as an employee earlier in my business strategy, now, get a chance.

And, to my bewilderment, some of the ones that I think will be the worst, turn out to be absolute champions. Some others, on whom I had banked very heavily, have jumped ship at the first storm.

After the initial training program of about three months, the great survivors are invited to graduate into our firm with the understanding that they are about to experience a unique voluntary system which thrives on freedom of choice and the priorities one places on his or her life.

The winners will achieve higher earnings in our firm than anywhere else, since their earnings are a direct reflection of their personal productivity. However, people with low ambition and production must reduce their working hours in order to comply with the minimum wage law.

This means, that eventually, the low producers will have to reduce the work hours close to zero, therefore phasing themselves out. Surely they will have learned from the experience and perhaps know how to treat the next chance more deservingly.

I cannot think of a more fair, more dignified reward system. Frankly, I am very proud of it. It leaves me with a clean conscience.

There is one other method of adding winners to a company's team. I discovered this method by examining some of my people who have been loyal to my company for many years.

How did my firm attract them? One of the best reservoirs for an effective staff are people who already have a job, such as people who call on or come to your office trying to sell you something or even clients.

Diane is one of my finest agents. She is celebrating her 12th anniversary with my firm. How did I find Diane?

Diane came to my office trying to sell me something. She did a superb job trying to convince me that I should move my operation to the real estate property her husband owned.

I was impressed with Diane's presentation and, as I got to know her, with her accomplishments in life. She was happily married to the same man for the past 25 years, which showed sound basic judgment, a sense of commitment, and the power to work out problems rather than run away from them.

Diane also had reared and inspired two successful daughters. Naturally, she has been very instrumental in the growth of Envoye Travel.

Pat is another great example. Prior to joining my firm, Pat was a client. She impressed me with the way she conducted her business and how she raised her family.

Pat was very organized and gave tremendous attention to details. I lured Pat into my firm by asking her to help out when she complained that an agent of mine had not returned her call.

Another resource for excellent employees are senior citizens. They are stable and responsible, offering both customer and job appreciation.

With the right combination of everything involved in running a business and the right employees, any travel agency should succeed.

It's not what you think! Taking the three day journey through the world's largest rainforest our bus was... fumigated.

# CHAPTER 10

# A NEW DIRECTION

*"A leader is one who knows the way, goes the way, and shows the way."* –John C. Maxwell

A successful leader is rooted in a philosophy that inspires and motivates others to personal growth and loyalty toward the common goal. The values of a leader's philosophy will draw individuals with similar ethics.

There is a desire in all of us to be proud of our leaders. A respected leader is more effective.

In order to maintain the necessary respect, the leader must live according to a high set of personal values and have knowledge of the industry he or she represents. The leader must set goals, values and rules, and have an understanding of which incentives will motivate a person the most.

The leader must create an environment that is desirable. There are more and more people who prefer a desirable office environment over a higher pay.

In both my personal and professional life, I have encountered a variety of leaders, each with his or her own style of leadership. Some were successful. Some were failures.

In the following pages, I will discuss several different leadership philosophies and how they apply to an office situation.

Leadership Based on Fear

The very first of all the different types of leaderships I experienced as a child was one based on fear. I grew up in Germany under Nazism, and its power was based on fear. Under the Nazis' iron rule, individual creativity and productivity turned stagnant.

Leadership based on fear, whether in government or in the business world, does not have a handle on success. Fear is an obstacle which freezes the potential of most people. It is self-defeating. It intimidates people to the extent that it keeps them from taking risks, assuming responsibilities, and even taking action.

Several years ago, I served as a tour guide to a large group of U.S. citizens visiting the Soviet Union. While there, we traveled on the Siberian Express. It was June and incredibly hot inside the train. The train did not have air conditioning and the windows were stuck.

A train conductor elbowed his way periodically through the crowded train. He had an arrogance about him, and his Stalin-styled moustache only added to this image.

As the conductor stopped in our compartment to check our visas, I asked him, as charmingly as possible, if he could please tell me how to open the windows so we could catch some cool air. He objected firmly to opening any windows. Everything was to remain as it was.

The conductor was afraid to make a decision about even something as minor as opening some sealed windows. Any decision changing a situation could get him into trouble. So, he tried to reason with me: "It gets cold in winter." He pointed at the window.

None of the Soviet passengers on the train dared to open the window either. They just sat there, sweat pouring from their foreheads and running down their temples.

When the perspiration reached the point of being unbearable, one young man peeled off his clothing right down to his sweat-drenched grey underwear. The other passengers watched him and then followed his example.

The American passengers reacted differently. No sooner did the conductor turn his back on them, they pulled out Swiss pocket knives and began to poke around the old putty-like substance that sealed the joints around each window.

By the time the conductor passed our compartment for the third time, the windows were wide open with the fresh air blowing vigorously.

Again the conductor was afraid to act. He pretended to be oblivious to the open windows.

The Russian passengers were amazed. They could not believe the initiative the Americans had displayed. Astounded, they watched as the Americans proceeded to pry open one window after another until all the windows were open.


Positive Leadership

The first sample of positive leadership that I received came from my mother.

My mother was not a much schooled person. She only had the standard, minimum school education that was traditional among the masses of her contemporaries. In time, she became one of the most knowledgeable persons I have ever known. She read constantly.

When I was a child, my mother and I often looked at pictures together. She could identify the cities of the world by their landmarks.

Mother could point at a picture of the Taj Mahal and say, "Someday I would like to visit Agra during a full moon when all the brilliant mosaics of the Taj Mahal are reflecting in the fountain and competing with the glitter of the stars."

Or, she would show me a picture of an Egyptian pyramid and say, "This is the oldest building in the world."

Mother would tell me about the Amazon and how it, at one time, flowed in the other direction and how it creates its own rain. She sparked my imagination.

As she told me about the places in the pictures, her remarks intrigued me and sparked my young imagination far more than the most fantastic fairy tales, or Star Wars. These were the first glimpses I had of the world beyond my own. They instilled in me the burning desire to someday catch up with her knowledge and maybe even to travel to all those far-away, spell-binding places.

She never once asked me to read books. She didn't have to. Her example inspired an unquenchable thirst for knowledge. I read every book I could get my hands on. And, I grew up believing that reading was my own idea.

Today, I realize that it was my mother who inspired my burning desire to read. She motivated me in the most effective of all possible ways: by making me think it was my own idea.

My mother was one of those outstanding leaders who was so involved in leading others to personal success that she never even realized what incredible leadership talents she possessed. Her gentle urging was almost on a subliminal level.

Mother inspired her children in a manner that went unnoticed because it was fun and was void of any force, criticism, or intimidation. Her method of leadership made success twice as alluring and desirable. Thank you, Mother.

I aspire to my mother's quiet type of leadership. Trying to adapt it and to exercise it in my firm remains a daily challenge. I have established maximum, individual freedom for everyone, and I try to inspire my staff with new ideas and incentives that spark their motivation.

Inspiration by Example

At age 16, I was exposed to another leader that made a major impact on my life. The credit goes to Herr Rudolph Mazijewski. He was my boss when I worked as an apprentice at Deiter, the oldest, most prestigious jewelry store in my hometown of Essen.

Herr Mazijewski spoke two foreign languages. Whenever a client from France or England conducted business with our firm, Herr Mazijewski was the person everyone had to depend on.

All of us were in awe that anybody could converse in a language other than their own. Herr Mazijewski greatly impressed me. His inspiration led me to believe that my advancement, both personal and professional, would be enhanced if I became fluent in the four major languages of the time: English, French, Spanish, and, of course, my own German.

I left Germany on my own at the age of 19 to live in different countries. It was the best and least expensive way of learning a language.

I worked mostly as a domestic just so I could learn the language in each country. Originally, my plan was to return to Essen one day and work at Deiter, helping tourists from other countries. However, once I began sampling the different attractions the world had in store for me, once I discovered the excitement of travel, I never returned to Essen again, except for short family visits.

Mr. Mazijewski's knowledge of languages was one more motivation for me to travel. Learning those other languages remains the biggest advantage I have today when I visit different cultures abroad.

It offers a much deeper, more intensive, and totally different travel experience.


Honorable Leadership

I have always gravitated toward knowledge and decency. I consider this the reason why my life went straight up and is exciting and filled with great, lasting friendships. So, it was no wonder that when I married at the careful age of 31, I married a man of great leadership. D.C., who is a biologist and recently retired from Texas Tech University, took control of the financial department of our firm. Over the years, D.C.'s leadership has been of tremendous help to me. It is cut and dried, and very easy to understand. But, to follow it is very difficult.

D.C.'s decisions are based on what is right. For D.C., there is no compromise. There is no twisting of the truth. His leadership is best demonstrated by an event that occurred early on in our business ownership. At the time, our employees were asking for desk calculators with paper tapes. The ones they had did not have a tape, making certain numbers difficult to keep up with.

It was a reasonable request. I called Texas Instruments, the company from which we had purchased our present models. I asked the salesman if the company would take the models we owned in trade for the new ones. My offer was rejected. Being the stubborn German mule I am, I hated to take no for an answer. I contacted a neighbor who was employed by T.I.

My friend said, "Just tell T.I. that your old calculators broke down. In cases like that, T.I. will take them back and replace them free of charge with the newest model."

Forgive me, but I was excited over the prospect of not having to spend money on new desk calculators. We never seemed to have enough money for all the new inventions from which a travel service could benefit.

The following morning during breakfast, D.C. and I were seated in our open-air patio of our lake front home. I bragged to D.C. about my great deal: 12 new desk calculators free of charge.

But, D.C. was not at all impressed. "I could never lower myself to do that," D.C. told me.

Then he folded the large white napkin, rose from his chair, kissed me good-bye, and thanked me for toasting English muffins.

He smiled, "You know, success is not as important as how you succeed."

My first reaction was shock. But by the time he was ready to leave for the office, a great pride had taken hold of me. I knew he was in a hurry - he always was. I started carrying the china into the kitchen.

As he drove off in his white Ford pickup, I stood in our driveway for a while. I looked after him until his car disappeared around the curve in the road. Then I went to our garden, picked a few cherry tomatoes from the vines, and walked down the gentle grass slope which leads to our private lake shore.

There was not another person in sight and I relished the solitude. I took a seat on the sun-bleached bench by a tall cottonwood. My thoughts were with D.C. in his pickup. He was probably at the bridge crossing the Brazos River by then.

It was still early in the morning. The sun had not yet risen from behind the straight west Texas canyon walls in the east. My office did not expect me for another two hours. I remembered that I still had to feed Josephine's dog.

Josephine was visiting her native home of England. Her house was right across the lake from ours. I could see it underneath a tall willow each time the wind moved the branches. Should I take the car and drive around the lake? Take the boat? I decided to swim instead.

The water was warm. It lacked the sparkling, drinking-water quality of the lakes I was used to in Germany. Lake Ransom Canyon had the coffee aux laity color of rivers in the tropics. The color stirred up memories of an old adventure on the Rio de la Platta which flows along the border between Argentina and Uruguay.

D.C.'s remark was still in my mind. "Success is not as important as how you succeed...I could not lower myself to do that."

What a great person D.C. was!

All that day D.C.'s remark remained on my mind. How lucky could I be to be married to a partner of his caliber? We might never be as wealthy as some, but I was by far more content, and I cherished the inner strength and self-confidence that derived from D.C.'s moral and ethical leadership.

I knew I lost a good deal on office machines, but I gained so much more. I gained another sample of D.C.'s integrity. He lived according to what he said he stood for. I knew I could always trust him. He was a man of honor.

Today, after 20 years in business, I am convinced that one reason why we have such great employees and why our business is doing well, is primarily attributed to D.C's high moral leadership.

There is no waste of time when D.C. makes a decision, no squandering of energy trying to beat the system, no finessing around someone.

He knows exactly what he wants, and he wants what is right. There are no compromises, no stretches of the truth.

When I grew up in Nazi Germany, I did not know that such tremendous inner power - both in business survival and reaching business goals - could flow from the truth.

The leader who decides according to high ethics has an inner peace and conviction that cannot be ruffled by any crisis. Knowing he is right gives him the advantage of the calmness that is needed to maintain control and make the right decisions.

This kind of leader is the true survivor!


The Undercover Leader

Over the years, I have discovered that the leadership in an organization does not always come from the boss.

We have people in our firm that exercise a strong leadership among their peers. These are the leaders others flock to, sometimes to get advice, sometimes for inspiration.

These undercover leaders are to be watched carefully. They can make or break a small firm.

I make special efforts to inspire them so they will have a positive outlook and act in support of the values I want installed in the company.


A Leader for All Reasons

A firm requires different styles of leadership as it grows through a variety of stages and faces specific situations. It is very much like a child growing up.

New on the job, the leader frequently spends an enormous amount of personal energy carrying an abundance of expectation, intolerance, and impatience.

Farther down the road of experience, the leader discovers that no matter what and no matter how severe a crisis, if you hang in there and give it your very best, you eventually will see your dream shine through.

Having learned his or her lessons, the now-seasoned leader has security and self-assurance. They begin to miss the excitement of a crisis, the panic and challenge.

In looking back, I would not want to change the course of events my firm went through. It eventually made Envoye Travel Service the unique company it is today.

A resilient, stable institution, Envoye Travel is disaster resistant with a sense of no-matter-what stability. All the mammoth crises of the past now surface only as memories of great tests which proved Envoye's tremendous strength and backbone for survival.

Envoye Travel reminds me of the big live oak which shades our farm house in Brazos County. The tree must have tremendous roots for it has survived so many storms. The roots of a firm are the leader's philosophy.


The Office without a Leader

Shortly after I moved our third office, Envoye Travel South, to its present location, circumstances led to a new experiment.

The office was without a manager, and I was not about to appoint a manager until the gross sales of that office approached five million dollars. Until that time, I decided, we would find out what an office would be like without a leader or manager.

To my surprise, the office did extremely well. As it turned out, we suddenly had several managers in the office. Every travel counselor became a manager.

Each counselor assumed responsibilities for the smooth operation of the office, with was no class distinction and no supervision. It was an enthusiastic, free-flowing office with sales on a steady incline.

Since everybody worked on a commission basis, retaining for themselves one-third of the commission they generated, everyone was interested in pleasing the clients. The client became everyone's boss.

Of course, I established general office rules, but these were kept to a minimum.

The first thing I noticed was that all of the agents made certain that their clients would receive the best service possible, even when the agent was not in the office.

To assure quality service, it was necessary for everyone to treat every client with the greatest courtesy, even the client of an absent agent. After all, there would come a time when every agent took a turn to be absent. And, one way to secure quality service during such a moment was to treat the clients of your colleagues as well as you would your own.

Office hours went to a maximum. When a sign painter carefully painted the official office hours on the glass entry door, travel counselor Pauline read them aloud in her Queens English, and everyone in the office laughed.

"8 a.m. to 9 p.m.! Why bother going home?" Pauline said with a chuckle. The benefit of the long hours were that every travel counselor could pretty much select the office hours they found best. As long as the office was manned by at least five agents until 5 p.m., we would be in excellent shape.

Shiny, a school teacher during the day, was very pleased to be able to work evenings in the agency. She also scheduled herself for Saturday and Sunday work. Judie, a night person by character, preferred arriving at the office early in the afternoon and working until 9 p.m.

And, I could jog in the mornings with D.C.'s two English pointers and my stray collie and then spend a few hours writing, before driving to the office and staying until closing time, which frequently was not until midnight.

The travel counselors among themselves decided which hours they would work during the month to come. One counselor at a time would assume responsibility for the work schedule. That responsibility changed periodically, giving everyone a sense of appreciation for the job of schedule planning.

The new rules to guarantee good customer service protection required that not more than two agents be out of the office at the same time. The person scheduled first to be off had the priority to be absent.

Additional office duties were handled on a volunteer basis and according to talent. Everyone was selected to take responsibility for specific office tasks.

The team of "self-appointed managers" even solved our old problem of filing, stamping, and reordering brochures. Lori and Marie Anne volunteered to take charge of that duty. It was a smart selection on their part, since brochures are our products and the person who files them always knows where to find the product and which products are new.

Deena and Inge, our two part-time bookkeepers, shared the duties of the financial department. Inge covered the morning hours, and Deena worked afternoons and Saturdays. If one of them chose to be absent for a few days, the other one worked additional hours. Basically, Inge was in charge of accounts payable, and Deena was in charge of accounts receivable.

Envoye Travel South is a true model office. It's a miracle of cooperation. There is a lot of enthusiasm in our office along with a healthy sense of humor and a sense of freedom and independence. Everyone is very responsible and looks after the customers' interest. Best of all the productivity is up and on a constant climb.

I enjoy tremendously going to the office, and my agents have told me on several occasions that they, too, cherish coming to work. This alone is an accomplishment of which I am very proud of.

My personal office is at Envoye Travel South mainly because of its longer-than-normal office hours and because it is open on Saturday and Sunday afternoon. I don't mind at all being in the office on those days. I don't feel justified asking anyone on my staff to work Sundays.

Maybe it's the leadership instinct in me which dictates that it would be unfair to expect anything of others that I am not willing to do myself. Not having a manager at Envoye Travel South makes it easy to involve every one of my staff at that office in two of the most important aspects of the free market economy: production and cost. I bring the effect of the free market economy to their personal doorsteps by giving them freedom of choice.

Each person has the freedom to decide how hard they wish to work. A person's production determines his or her rewards, such as the size of their paycheck, who gets the most spacious office, the free trip, and so forth.

Remember, there is not a person in this world who can be pushed to maximum success - just like there is no way to hold back a person who is determined to succeed!

Developing Your Own Personal Leadership Style

As your experience level grows, you will develop your own personal leadership style.

In the meantime, you may find that different situations call for different leadership styles. It is possible to incorporate all of these styles into your leadership style. Even leadership by fear, although not recommended, might be used on occasions. But, in that circumstance, remember that it is not a successful leadership style.

When placed in a situation where leadership by fear seems to be the only solution, you should re-evaluate the level of contribution to your firm by the employee who necessitates your use of leadership by fear.

Keep these different styles in mind when you start your travel agency business because your leadership style can make or break your business. Remember that you must set an example through your leadership which your employees can respect!

# CHAPTER 11

# THE GOOD & BAD

*"Our talent for providing service is measured by how
much we care for the benefit of our fellow men."*

What makes someone a champion in service? What makes someone a
great quarterback? Talent and practice.

Our talent for providing service is measured by how much we care
for the benefit of our fellow men. I cared a tremendous amount. And
practice? For 50 years I have practiced with the finest teams in the service
industry.

Prior to my present affiliation with American Express, I enjoyed
the distinct honor of being employed by several of the leading service
companies in the world -Deiter, Vacheron et Constantin, Tiffany's, and
Gumps.

Each one of these prestigious companies pursues an exceptionally
high standard of customer service. Their clients represent the most
complex, most knowledgeable, most demanding consumers on the face
of this earth. Kings, queens, heads of governments, the role models of our
society, were among our clients.


Service: An International Language

I remember one of my colleagues at Deiter waiting on Frau Berta
Krupp von Bohlen and Halbach. The conversation was in the second
person. It was channeled elegantly though one of Frau Krupp's
accompanying ladies. I watched and listened in fascination.

My first opportunity to be actively involved in superior service happened when I was about 15 years old. From ages 14 to 17, I was an apprentice at Deiter.

Hans Lupner, my boss, asked me to hand-deliver a wristwatch that had just been repaired by the masters at Deiter. The client, a family named Birkenhauer, lived in a fashionable suburb on the outskirts of Essen. It took me two hours to reach the Birkenhauer home, and two hours to return. I journeyed by trolley and walked through a rainstorm until I finally stood dripping wet in the entry hall of the elegant home.

The young man who received me, was the most handsome man I had ever encountered. That I fell madly in love didn't matter to anyone but me, and I kept it my secret. The only thing that did count was that the Deiter client received the watch one day before it was promised, rainstorm or not.

I was so honored and deeply impressed that my boss at Deiter had selected me from among all the other apprentices in the firm to perform the "important" job. And, my young vanity calculated that my boss must have thought I would make the best impression on the client. I was as wet as an otter and as cocky as a rooster. My self-esteem rose by several degrees.

While working at Vacheron et Constatin in Geneva, Switzerland, a colleague of mine and I, one afternoon, struggled to get a heavy suitcase filled to the top with platinum and diamond watches across the street and over the bridge on the Rhone river to the Hotel Des Bergues. Our client, a king, expected us.

His Royal Highness liked Vacheron ET Constantin watches. He purchased them as souvenirs for his friends. To give each watch his personal touch, he requested that our firm, transfer a replica of his portrait to the face of each watch. The job was a remarkable undertaking during the conservative trend of the 1950's in Switzerland in an ultra-conservative firm like Vacheron & Constantin.

As we were leaving the hotel, a reporter stopped me to find out more about our visit. But, confidentiality was part of our good service!

Service in the Travel Industry

As an American Express Representative office, we received a call from an American Express cardholder one night. The card holder was calling from the Lubbock jail. She had been arrested and taken to the jail after she was stopped by a police officer who discovered that she had not paid an old traffic ticket. The woman was from out of town and did not have enough money to take care of the fine or to post bond.

But, she did have an American Express Credit Card. My office carried the necessary amount of Traveler's Cheques to the jail, and she was on her way.

One of the most exceptional scenarios of good service happened in my office when Bob Hall suddenly had to fly on business to India. Debra sent Mr. Hall's passport to the Indian Embassy, requesting a visa. One day prior to Mr. Hall's departure his passport and visa still had not yet been returned to our office.

There was only one thing to do: Debra flew from Lubbock to Washington, D.C., picked up Mr. Hall's passport and visa at the Indian Embassy, and then met Mr. Hall at the airport in Dallas just before his Lufthansa flight, via Frankfurt, to Delhi.

Debra's service was particularly remarkable since she missed a date that night with her husband-to-be. They had planned to look at wedding rings!

Good Service Keeps Good Customers

Good service is the difference between success and failure. It costs five times more to recruit a new client than it does to keep a present one.

We must remember that the client always wins because all the client has to do is contact another travel service. You know that when the client comes to you, the client already knows where he or she wants to go and how much money he or she intends to spend.

What the client has not yet decided on is WHO will be the travel agent!

Communicate your interest in the client's welfare by volunteering valuable pointers like: "Be sure to plan your departure on a Tuesday or Thursday because the airfares are usually lower on those days."

Or, advise a honeymoon couple to get married on a Friday instead of a Saturday so they can take advantage of all the great packages that depart on Saturday mornings!

Good Service Means Pleasing the Client

Success is measured on our ability to please and to befriend the most challenging among our clients as well as by our effectiveness to supply what the client wants. The degree to which we benefit our clients directly reflects the same as to how we benefit the company we work for.

In the challenging world of free enterprise and service, we are constantly surrounded by the few who succeed and by the masses who don't. Those who succeed have the commitment to get their clients what they need.

It's the Little Things That Count

Providing good service often does not cost the company any extra money. Usually it is the small, seemingly insignificant touches that make the best impression on the clients.

Good service means:
* Listening carefully to what the client has to say.
* Answering all the questions a customer has.
* Throwing in that extra information about which the client might not have thought to ask.
* Getting the brochures to the client the same day the client requests them.
* Being sensitive to the client's needs and providing more than the client expects.
* Putting the brochures the clients select in an easy-to-carry bag.
* Talking in a tone of voice that inspires the client rather than one that creates a feeling of having reached a dead-end street.
* Offering your client a cool glass of water.

Doing a few things such as those listed above could set you miles apart from your competitor who just hands the client a brochure and sends him on his way.

I have sold many trips to clients who came to my office with a brochure from a rival travel agency!

The reason I receive the clients' business is because I am hospitable, offering the clients a seat and taking the time to visit with them.

## Every Client is Worth Your Time

Never write off a client, expecting him or her to be just a shopper. Each and every shopper can be converted into a client by a talented, caring salesperson who has the right attitude.

Success in a service industry is measured by our ability to supply the client with more then what the client wants.

## Going the Extra Mile in the Name of Service

Not everyone has the same desire to please the customer, and, in our business, we often have to make up the slack left by not-so-conscientious people.

For a trip on which I was escorting 50 people to Orlando, Florida, I made arrangements for a tour guide to meet our group at the airport.

On the bus ride to our hotel, I urged the tour guide to please start talking and entertaining our group. But, the young woman would not follow my suggestions. She just sat there, and the only talking she did was directed at the bus driver.

Embarrassed that I was responsible for this tour, I took over the microphone and started talking. I did not know anything about Florida or Orlando, so I started telling travel jokes and talked about my travel experiences.

That night, I studied the history of Florida and Orlando in my hotel room. The local telephone book gave me a history on the city and its founder. Early the next morning I went through some of the gift shops in the hotel, asking the employees about their life in Florida.

It was that telephone-book history and the employees' stories that I repeated to the bus passengers. Everyone had a wonderful time and wanted to go on the next tour I was scheduled to "conduct."

It just took a little extra work on my part to provide for my clients what the tour guide was not offering. I got the repeat customers! I doubt that she will.

## Beware the Con Artist

As a business owner or employee, there are several customer situations to be especially wary of:

Imagine that you have a very important client. The client gives your company a considerable amount of business, taking first class trips to Saudi Arabia several times a year, usually several people traveling together.

For the past two years, the client has always paid his bills promptly. It's an oil company in Saudi Arabia that reimburses the travelers. They don't use credit cards. They don't care for them, the client explains.

Then one Friday afternoon, just before your office closes and after the banks are already closed, the client comes to your office with an emergency. They need 10 first class tickets to Saudi Arabia on the first flight in the morning.

The client asks for a considerable amount of Travelers Cheques. The client pays with a personal check. No problem. The client has been so nice and dependable. The client's checks were always covered before.

On Monday, the client's check bounces. The Travelers Cheques are all cashed in. The client is gone for good.

Lesson learned? Never ever trust a business traveler who does not care for credit cards. Run a credit check on the client - maybe a credit card company has withdrawn the membership from the client.

And, never take a risk on a client's good conduct with your firm. It might all be part of the game to gain your confidence.

Thefts often occur on weekends, and, usually, the thief is an expert in instilling confidence and compassion in the victim.

I remember the Saturday on which I sold, or rather gave away, several high-dollar airline tickets to a client who wanted to fly his children to visit their sick mother. He paid with an impressive company check. The check was part of a large spreadsheet. All expenses were listed carefully.

Everything looked so right. So official. A company check. And, the poor children wanting to see their sick mother!

Well, the check bounced. The address on the check was incorrect. So was the driver's license which was so efficiently printed on the checks. The company was out of business.

Lesson learned? I should have referred the client to the airline for the purchase of the tickets. Of course, airlines would not have accepted his check.

Another Saturday turned infamous when two clients paid cash for several thousand dollars' worth of Travelers Cheques. During the transaction, the phone rang. The agent picked up the phone. Someone wanted to know our office hours and how to get to our office from downtown. The distracting phone call was part of the setup, but the agent of course did not know that.

Carefully, the agent instructed the client on how to drive to our office. While she talked, she placed the cash in a drawer and handed the Travelers Cheques to the clients.

After the clients left, the agent went to place the money in the safe. When she opened the drawer, the money was gone. And, so were the Travelers Cheques. Apparently the thieves watched carefully where the agent put the cash and the Travelers Cheques.

The agent called American Express and was able to put an alert on the Travelers Cheques. Since the thieves had not had time to cash in the Travelers Cheques, she was able to cancel their validity. And, because the checks were canceled, our firm did not actually lose any money from the theft. However, the potential for loss was tremendous.

Lesson learned? When you deal with cash, or travelers checks, never, not even for a second, allow anyone or anything distract your attention. Keep your hands and your mind on the valuables in front of you at all times.

This warning should keep you and your employees on your toes.

However, please remember that, fortunately, most customers are NOT thieves. All who enter the doors of your business should be treated responsibly, yes, but also they should be treated with courtesy and respect!

Sigrid- an immigrant dreaming of a better future in America.

# CHAPTER 12

# OFFICE ENVIRONMENT

*"All people become a team where there is gentleness."*

Many of the people in today's work force spend more time at work than they do at home. Yet, they create a great home environment. So, why should they settle for a second-class office environment? It doesn't make sense, does it?

An office environment should be more than just some carefully placed chairs and the right shade of carpet or even expensive art objects. While the ideal office *should* be functional, practical, well-organized, logical, clean, fun, and inspiring, the ideal office environment is much more than this.

A productive environment is not something co-workers *find* at the office when they arrive, but something that they *bring* to the office with them. The ideal office environment consists of workers that are not only flexible, respectful, and understanding, but also inspiring. The ideal office should be a place to look forward to every day, not just because of the pleasant surroundings, but also because of the attitude of the people who work there.

In order to maintain such a desirable environment, each office member must volunteer their participation. This is easy to accomplish if each member realizes that their personal contributions serve their own best interests. A pleasant, productive office environment inspires customer confidence and jets each of its architects toward success.

That my office has a pleasant, flexible, and, sometimes, unusual environment was never more evident than the day my family arrived from Germany to investigate my travel agency. The same day they arrived in Lubbock, I invited them to spend the day in my office.

117

On that particular day, things in the office were a bit *cuckoo*. Pat arrived in the office with a turkey under her arm explaining that her oven at home had broken down and that she was going to cook her family's dinner in our office oven. Angela had brought a basket full of kittens for which she hoped to find owners during the course of the day. Fran took out her upper dentures while she devoured the breakfast doughnuts. And, Lucy ran sobbing through the office searching for a substantial cruise deposit she had misplaced.

During our drive home that night, my family had a good laugh at the day's events and swore that the situations they had witnessed that day could never have happened in a German company. I didn't say anything because I knew that the next day - Halloween - would be even more unusual for my guests from Germany. They do not celebrate Halloween in Germany.

The next morning my visitors were preparing for another day observing the travel agency business. My sister Monika and my cousin Herbert were sitting around the breakfast table with some of my other relatives. I walked into the breakfast room dressed in the outfit of a German military general - boots, knickers, steel helmet, ornaments, and sword.

"You must be kidding," Monika said. Herbert just chuckled.

I played the game well. I didn't say a word and I tried to behave as normally as possible.

At the office, Ann was wearing a green surgical suit. Her name tag read "Doctor Strange Love," and a syringe was sticking out of her pocket. Larry was dressed like an Indian warrior with a feathered headband and war paint. At the front desk, Jane sat with a dozen balloons knotted to her mini dress. The button she wore identified her as the "First Woman Astronaut."

"Things like this just would not be possible in Germany," Herbert said, shaking his head. "Well, at my agency, having fun at work is as important as working," I explained. "I want my agents to look forward to coming to work each day. It's their environment, and as long as the sales of the present year are higher than those of the previous year, personal freedom is justified. And, we can afford to act 'Lolo' (which means 'stupid' in Pelegrina) once in a while."

The following days were more in keeping with normal business traditions, but my German visitors were still amazed at how casual our office environment was and how everyone seemed to get along quite well.

It was hard for them to understand that I could run a successful business without the restrictions they expected.

My family was in awe of the positive atmosphere. "Sigrid," my sister questioned, "What is your recipe to such an amazing environment?" Our office uses the perfect formula, my husband D.C. has for a productive office environment: It is important that we treat each person, whether customer or co-worker, with respect and that we are careful never to destroy anyone's dignity. It is not important whether we like or dislike our colleagues. On the other hand, if two people in a company do not get along, and cannot treat each other with respect, it can adversely affect the entire firm. Oh and I almost forgot! We laugh a lot, and we discovered that humor solves most problems.


You Create Your Own Environment

The day I took my family back to the airport for their flight back to Germany, I was a bit homesick. As an immigrant, you always sit between two chairs - some of the time you long for the place where you are not.

I am fortunate because I enjoy the country of my choice. But, on my drive back from the airport, my thoughts circulated around Germany and how the experiences of my childhood there often crept into my business life here in the United States, from the influence of the war to the influence of my mother, from my love of travel burgeoning out of the need to work to bringing "Stimmung" as a hostess gift in lieu of a more traditional gift.

In Germany, if you went to someone's home, you brought a small gift - a bouquet of flowers, a tray of homemade cookies, or some other small remembrance. However, right after World War II, Germans were too poor to comply with such kind traditions.

One of the fringe benefits of poverty can be creativity. My mother created a wonderful substitute for the hostess gifts we could not afford. As it turned out, the substitute was a far more attractive and a much more appreciated gift than any material thing we could have brought. My mother inspired us children to bring *Stimmung* as our hostess gift.

*Stimmung* is difficult to translate into English, but, loosely, it means an upbeat mood, a desirable atmosphere, or ambiance which leads to a special environment.

Mother told us that each of us could make the difference in the mood of the other guests each time we were invited to a party. She told us that each of us had the chance to make the environment at the party the most desirable one possible.

Right before we knocked on the front door, my mother would remind us one more time by saying, "Remember, smile. We are bringing *Stimmung.*"

Soon, the awareness of how great our personal influence actually could be spread from parties to time spent in school and from school to our home life and jobs. Each of us knew that wherever we were, we could make the difference. It was we who were in control of the environment around us.

We were responsible for how the people around us felt, and there was nothing magical about it. All we had to do was show a sense of humor, be kind and helpful to others, and be tolerant of how others treated us.

My mother was the master in creating a desirable environment no matter what the circumstances. So, to this day, I try to remember my mother's shining philosophy. I remind myself every day on the way in to the office: "Remember, Sigrid, smile. You must bring *Stimmung.*"

You Can't Afford Complainers

Although I have tried my best to bring a pleasant and inspiring attitude with me to work, the members of my staff weren't always as well versed in the ways of *Stimmung* as they are now.

As D.C. says, the ideal office environment depends on *everyone* in the office. A productive, harmonious office environment is as much a reflection of each member of the office as a clean residential area reflects the priorities of each resident.

"Life isn't fair," my mother used to say. "Be glad that it isn't. If life were fair, none of us would have as good a deal as we have."

Complaining and blaming others when things became upsetting was beneath my mother's dignity. In fact, I cannot remember my mother ever complaining even when she had cause.

I am certain that with four children and nothing to eat, my mother must have had some terrible times. But, she never complained about them. If she did not feel on top of the world, nobody knew it. To talk about unpleasant matters just wasn't ladylike or gentlemanly in our home.

Eventually my mother died of cancer. None of us knew about her tragic disease until one month before her death when the pain was so severe that she was finally admitted to the hospital. It was still she who cheered us on. She died as she had lived, a lady who put others first.

Armed with inspiration from my mother and D.C.'s wisdom, I have often listened to the complainers among my staff and wondered how most effectively I could make them realize that it takes less energy to examine yourself and the issue and take action to improve the situation than it does to spend all day complaining about particular circumstances.

An inspiration of how to improve complainers' attitude came to me during a flight to Miami. In the Delta Airlines' flight magazine was an article featuring a company whose profits had soared after the owner introduced to his staff a four-way test of improving office environment. I copied the four-way test, scribbling the rules on the back of my boarding pass, and posted them later, for maximum visibility, on the bulletin board in our office bathroom.

The four-way test helps a person decide whether or not something should be said aloud. Before complaining or fussing, individuals ask themselves if what they are about to say passes these four tests:

*1) Is it the truth?*
*2) Is it fair to all concerned?*
*3) Will it build goodwill and better friendship?*
*4) Is it beneficial to all concerned?*

I added my own note alongside the four-way test:
*Thanks to all of you who have actively shared in promoting a desirable office environment!*

* *It works doesn't it - not to show favoritism toward*
    *any particular colleague?*
* *I am proud of all of you who realize, that in the*
    *event of an office crisis, it is important that you ask*
    *yourself, "What could I have done to avoid the crisis."*
    *And, "what can I do to solve the crisis?"*
* *Our quality as a person is best judged by the environment we manage*
    *to create around us. How about you? Do people exposed to your*
    *behavior blossom or do they wilt?*

* *True business sophistication is to take different*
  *colleagues to lunch - especially those you have an axe to grind with.*
  *By taking to lunch the person with whom you feel*
  *least at ease, you might bring about a pleasant turn*
  *in your relationship.*
* *It is wise to remember that we come to the office to*
  *pursue our professional dreams. We expedite our goals by engaging in*
  *productive activities.*
* *It is the calling of a leader to be smart with*
  *personal time as well as being considerate by not*
  *wasting the time of your co-workers. By placing the*
  *interest of your co-workers first, you will end up the real winner.*
* *We must be grateful for all clients. Each one provides us with the*
  *opportunity of holding*
  *our job and bringing us one step closer to our dream.*
* *Criticism can be productive, but only if it is self-*
  *criticism. Should two people engage in a conflict, remember what is*
  *at stake. The entire office will suffer.*
* *Have you ever regretted something you did not say?*
  *Have you ever noticed that positive comments invite*
  *positive comments? And, negative comments foster*
  *negative comments?*

The note on the bathroom wall, believe it or not, helped to create a better atmosphere.

## A New Kind of Office Management

I realized that as the leader of our office and president of my company, I should be the person who demonstrates the highest commitment toward creating a productive office environment. However, the model environment demands the direct involvement and contribution of each office member, not just an owner trying to set a good example.

With that in mind, I decided to have the office staff elect the next office manager. One evening before leaving the office, I placed a memo on each staff member's desk. The memo referred to the importance of protecting our positive, general office goals. The memo also urged each staff member to turn in a list with the qualities they wished to see represented in a future office manager.

I wasn't surprised when I read the responses. Everyone wished to have a manager who was positive, inspiring, dependable, well-informed, honest, on-time, organized, neat, and who worked the hours as scheduled and also pitched in with the extra office work whenever needed.

The individual responses to my memo turned out to be a wonderful, discreet opportunity to air what most employees did not appreciate in their co-workers' habits. Also, for those on the staff who aspired to be elected as office manager, the list of qualities made them aware of the characteristics they needed to possess in order to obtain the endorsement of their colleagues. And, by bringing these qualities to their attention, the final choice would be fair.

Each staff member who considered himself or herself a candidate for the position used the opportunity for an indirect campaign to become manager.

They all developed and demonstrated the mandatory manager's characteristics. The office environment improved daily and sales soared. Our office even began receiving compliments both from customers and from within our own ranks. I realized that I didn't deserve the credit for our pleasant atmosphere. It was the contribution from everybody in the office that created the pleasant atmosphere, and everybody deserved the applause.

I thanked the entire staff for the improvement, and we never elected a new manager! We all celebrated by having a Mexican lunch catered to the office. Afterwards, everyone was eager to join in and clean up the mess in our office *kitchen*.

It was a great sensation to develop a successful new style of management. The democratic style of management, where everyone is eager to contribute as if it were their own company, works for us, and it will work for your agency when used in combination with the other management and organizational techniques I discuss in this book.

Our new computer system includes memos. Instead of memos getting lost on cluttered desks, automation has brought the benefit of better communication between company members. Any staff member can now que a message to any other staff member, replacing paper notes of messages. The computer makes it easier for a democratic style of management to work because it keeps communication lines open.

Jointly, the staff also created a company manual establishing laws that benefitted all. I asked everyone to submit suggestions for company policies to one key office member who had a particular talent in computer science.

That person entered the policies into a star in the computer. The policies were reviewed by everyone and voted on. If the majority approved the suggestion, it became an office law.

Now, not only the office management but also the office manual were the products of the democratic form we found so successful in the agency. By making the creation of new office laws a joint project, all members took a greater interest in finding out about office laws and in seeing to it that they were enforced.


You Can't Buy Feelings

Some of life's most valuable lessons I've learned in my travels to the so-called *uncivilized* places - those places which have less emphasis on technology, fewer buttons to push, and more human touch than my own culture has. A splendid example was my trip to the South Pacific in the late 1970's as a guest of American Express.

The environment on the island of Bora Bora, from my point of view, was beautiful. My bungalow at the Hotel Bora Bora was set on stilts above a spectacular coral reef. To reach my bungalow, I took an inspiring walk across a long, narrow bridge which spanned the brilliant blue water of the South Pacific, starting on a white sandy beach and ending right at the door of my bungalow.

Although my bungalow was without television, radio, air conditioning, or even a telephone, I was not without entertainment. Inserted into the floor next to my bed was a large piece of glass that offered a spectacular view of the coral reef and all its marine life below. A flip of the switch near my bed illuminated the whole underwater paradise beneath my cabin. All night long I was fascinated by fish in all imaginable colors and the giant clams feeding endlessly.

The hotel offered other entertainment as well. A great island band performed on Wednesdays and Saturdays before dinner.

"They come every week," the manager told me. "I only hired one, and I only pay for one. The other eight are friends of the one I pay.

"They love to come out here and play their instruments together. They love this place for its atmosphere. Some competitors of mine tried to hire the whole band, but they prefer to come here. For the feeling, I guess. You can't buy feelings."

Although I have yet to find employees who will work for me for free because of the great atmosphere, my Bora Bora experience taught me that the way a person feels about a job is extremely more important than the money.

The salaries might be similar at other travel agencies. The difference at Envoye Travel is the environment. You must strive to make the environment of your offices as beautiful as the Hotel Bora Bora. Remember, *you can't buy feelings...*

CHAPTER 13

# KEYS TO MOTIVATION

*"Leaders must be close enough to relate to others, but far enough ahead to motivate them."* –John C. Maxwell

If my husband D.C. were to write this chapter on motivation, it would consist of two short sentences: "Motivation is an individualized phenomenon. It starts when the person gets up in the morning."

The most challenging test I face daily goes beyond my personal motivation. The real challenge is motivating the people around me. Employee motivation is particularly important to me because I realize that productive employees are the greatest capital your company can have.

The effect of one unmotivated employee can be as disastrous to your sales as one uncommitted worker can be to your office environment. An unmotivated employee can cause your company incredible losses just as a motivated employee can benefit your company beyond your wildest dreams.

Motivation, Goals, and Incentives

In general, I see motivation as the energy that propels us toward a goal. I see the incentive as the goal.

It takes tremendous energy to propel a rocket toward a star, just as it takes tremendous motivation to reach the incentive shining ahead. We have to bring our energy level up to our maximum potential if we desire to reach our incentive.

In other words, we have to give it our very best. And our very best can only be achieved if we keep our minds and bodies in the absolute best possible shape. D.C. is right: motivation is an individual characteristic. However, to many behavioral experts motivation is not only an individual characteristic, but also a cultural one.

Motivation in Different Cultures

Different personalities and different societies around the world are motivated by different incentives. Perhaps the finest example of this difference is this true story that takes us to Tahiti...

In Tahiti, near the shores of a black sand beach, a large, western-owned hotel chain decided to build a major hotel. Once the hotel was near completion, its western management did what was normal: it advertised to attract good employees, offering salaries that were the best in the islands. But...surprise! No applicants. The western managers even raised the salaries, yet still no applicants. Finally, a local, non-western person was consulted. A new ad went to press. This time the promise was: "A transistor radio for each employee."

Voila! The next day applicants lined up for hours sweating under a hot sun. Shortly thereafter, the employees, who now owned their transistor radios, stayed home again. A new incentive had to be found. Eventually, the western management ran out of incentives to motivate people in a society in which most members were perfectly satisfied to live in a modest home with plenty of time to go fishing.

Whenever I am in Tahiti, I check on the fate of the magnificently designed hotel. It has changed management quite a few times.

The Society Islands in the South Pacific are a wonderful place for social studies, simply because their people act differently from what we expect. One of my absolute favorite recollections is tied to the filming of a Hollywood movie. A film company experienced a motivation dilemma similar to the dilemma the hotel chain faced, but the film company was able to solve their problem just long enough to finish their film.

For the set of the film, the director needed beautiful, smiling south sea maidens. However, all of the beautiful maidens he found were toothless. The director solved the problem in Hollywood style, and dozens of sets of magnificent teeth were assembled in Hollywood and rushed to the Society Islands.

But, the next day, after all the wonderful teeth were distributed, not one maiden showed up for work. Hollywood had created the perfect incentive for the girls to stay home. Now that the girls had such ravishing smiles, they all shopped for husbands.

The Hollywood moguls scratched their heads and finally found the right motivation. The next group of smiling maidens they hired had to check in their Hollywood teeth each night before leaving the set. Eventually the maidens were allowed to keep their Hollywood dentures, but only if they showed up for work each day and only after all the filming was over.

When I first heard this wonderful story, I never thought in my wildest dreams that the day would come when these delightful tales would serve me as a perfect example of how important it is that, prior to motivating others, we find the right incentive. For my business, I have found a successful combination of recognition and incentives help keep my employees motivated.

And, what about our individual motivations? Wouldn't the world be a wonderful place if our highest incentive, our personal goal, was honor?

Consider Japan. In Japan, the manager is motivated by honor. If the company, which is in his trust, loses money, he feels compelled to correspondingly reduce his salary.

Come to think of it, the next time we feel threatened by Japanese products invading our economy, we might want to face up to the fact that, ultimately, honor always wins. Greed does not.

Freedom as Motivation

It took me twenty years in the travel business to finally accept my staff and to adjust my expectations according to each individual's motivation to stay with and excel in my company. "Remember," I tell my staff frequently, "I give you all the opportunities, but personal success is up to you."

Provided each person in my company has reached reasonable productivity and our office is manned sufficiently, then, yes, Peter could take the familiarization trip to London, and Lisa can go home every day at 3 p.m. Judy can enjoy the freedom to come and go as she pleases and work alone in the office all night. And, of course, Ruth can arrive at the office before 8 a.m. and leave before 5 p.m. And, Mary can branch off into outside sales. Mary actually pushes herself more now as an outside salesperson than she did as an inside salesperson. Her productivity has tripled. I believe having freedom of choice was a major factor in helping Mary find her own best schedule and, therefore, was a huge part of her success story.

In my first years of owning a travel agency, I ruled my business with an iron fist. After all, I was it. I was the boss. And, I had the highest motivation of anyone in the agency, higher than any member of my staff.

I remember getting goose bumps when an agent of mine took the liberty of addressing a client by his or her first name. The same thing happened to me when I overheard another agent of mine, Shiny, a pleasant, middle-aged lady originally from Korea, spell the name Ward with a very heavy oriental accent: "W as in watermelon, A as in apple tree, R like rosebushes and D...let's see, D for dogwood tree."

Since than I have learned to be less critical and to look at things with a sense of humor. I prefer to see my agents as my friends. Being sensitive to my employees' preferences has had the added bonus for me of increasing my joy in ownership.

A softer touch and listening to their ideas has produced a readiness in my co-workers to assume personal responsibilities. This readiness to assume responsibility is, of course, the inseparable by-product of freedom.

Suddenly new deliveries of brochures have stopped piling up. They are all neatly stamped, filed, and updated. The general office is kept tidy, has a personal touch, and is decorated with an inspiring and colorful array of travel artifacts.

Our office is covered at all times. Staff members assume the responsibility themselves to work out a schedule that benefits all.

By acknowledging the personal motivations of my employees, I discovered the most motivating incentive, the goal which appeals to all: FREEDOM. I suppose you could say freedom in the office is like the democratic form of government, whether it's used as motivation to increase sales or as an incentive to attain a pleasant environment.

If you decide to use freedom as a motivation for your employees, you will discover that it works. No matter how undesirable a job might be, if it allows for personal freedom, most people will be motivated to stay with the job and to do it well.

People simply perform better and produce more under freedom than under coercion. This was one of the many things I learned first-hand as a child in war-torn Nazi Germany. Freedom provides a sense of personal dignity, a taste of self-assurance and the fulfillment that comes with assuming responsibility for one's actions.

## Freedom for Your Managers

Freedom is a very productive motivator for my managers as well as general agents. Each one has been loyal to my company for many years. I am aware that several of my competitors have repeatedly made attractive job offers to them, only to find out that they cannot be bought. Their loyalty is with my company, and I highly appreciate this.

Diane, one of my managers, confirmed the success of the freedom approach when she told me, "Your trust in me is what I cherish. It makes it very attractive to work for you. It keeps me on my toes. It inspires me not to disappoint you. I wouldn't be the great coach I am, if someone else called the shots. I feel as though it was your recognition of my good leadership that gave me the freedom to call my own shots in my own office."

Doris, another one of my managers, said, "Sigrid, I want to thank you for all the confidence you have shown in me over the years. The very fact that you give me the freedom to manage your branch office as if it were my very own makes me feel responsible - as if it were indeed my own. If anything, I probably feel even more responsible toward your office, simply because it is yours, and I don't want to break your trust."

## Combining Recognitions and Travel Incentives
## As Motivations for Employees

Besides freedom, there are two other effective means for motivating employees. There are simple recognitions for jobs performed well, for high sales figures, for excellence of any kind. Aside from this psychological incentive, I see the need for a tangible incentive to propel employee motivation.

Recognitions and incentives do not have to be elaborate or costly in order to motivate effectively. In fact, they can be of no cost to the company and still be very effective.

The human desire for recognition is a very effective motivator. Periodically, I supply each member of my sales staff with a computer printout listing the agent's contribution to the company's profit. Profit, or an agent's contribution to the company's operational expenses, is a reflection of an agent's commission generated minus earnings and other capital benefits received.

Recognition, by itself, is a motivation to employees. I discovered that when I recognized, that attaching the personal productivity printouts to my employees' paychecks had a positive effect on sales. Each printout carries my personal message in the form of a drawing. Depending on the individual's production, I draw either a smiling face or a sad face.

Since I began distributing the printouts, there has never been an agent who doesn't look at the type of drawing first and the paycheck amount second. I guess my little drawing of a face is sort of like a Japanese character in that it conveys the message in a concentrated form and says it in the most gentle and effective fashion possible.

I also believe in using tangible incentives to motivate my employees. Once a year, five travel agents and one accountant get to take an office trip to one of the most popular vacation destinations in the world, with all expenses paid.

Our office celebrates the winners with a sort of "Oscar" Award. Our "Oscar" is very special. It's the incentive of our society of travel agents: a free first-class trip.

Qualifying for the award requires exceptional personal motivation. But, like most things in life, it isn't easy. Winning requires a commitment to hard work.

The "Oscar" is available to all, but only obtainable by those with the highest motivation. At year's end, I recognize the top five agents in my organization and together we jet off to enjoy ourselves and to find out if we can recommend the resort to our clients.

In addition to the top five salespeople, I invite one accountant to join in the fun. The accountant who qualifies for the trip is the one representing the branch office with the highest contribution to the company's bank account. After instigating the latter motivation, our company's expenditures went down considerably, and paper clips and note pads became collector's items.

Sigrid Carter

Travel As a Universal Motivation

What motivates us? Some may consider my answer unrealistic. I think that in our society, the single, most desirable, tangible incentive that motivates our actions is travel.

Companies offer incentive trips to their employees and customers much more frequently now than in the past. And, the incentive of travel, as a staff motivator, is particularly logical and effective on people who have chosen the travel industry as their line of work. I believe that it is possible to cure America's ills through motivation and incentives, including such nagging problems as illicit drugs, unemployment, and national debt.

I don't want to sound absurd, but how do you think high school students would react if, upon graduation, they could qualify for a free senior trip simply by passing a test proving they are drug free?

Maybe the senior trip could be financed by local businesses? Upon realizing the sociological benefits, airlines and hotels might cooperate by offering incentive rates. Companies participating in the sponsorship of the trips might qualify themselves for a tax reduction.

And, how do you suppose the chronically unemployed could be motivated? Those who could find a job, but, for one reason or another, don't? Maybe your idea is better than mine. You are welcome to laugh at mine.

Here is an example of how this could work using trips as the incentives. I recommend that the unemployed be offered the incentive of a trip.

Yes, after they have worked and paid taxes for at least one year and they are back into the routine of being productive members of our society, they would qualify. The luxury of the trip could be determined by the amount of taxes paid. What an incentive! What a motivation!

And who do I suppose will pay for the trip? One weekly welfare check that the unemployed person currently receives could finance the trip. And, even if two weekly or one monthly welfare check were needed for a one-week Caribbean Cruise, the government would still save by receiving income taxes from an individual who no longer roams the streets in discontent but instead is on cloud nine, working toward an incentive. What a wonderful motivation!

And, look at the fringe benefit. Look at the incredible potential. Educating people through travel. All we have to do is find the right incentive in order to motivate a person.


There Is No Such Thing As Failure

Philosophically, there is no failure. Philosophically, there are only learning experiences. Yet, many people fail over and over again. Why?

The people I know who have failed over and over again in one effort after another have two things in common: They are intelligent enough to risk trying, but they are too emotional to succeed.

These people make decisions based on their emotions and not their intelligence. They believe in excuses in spite of the fact that only their mothers will listen to their excuses.

For example, over dinner last night, Susan told me why her travel agency had failed:

"Right from the start, I didn't have the money for an accountant. My own time was barely enough for sales."

"I had a great talent for sales. My new business was growing by leaps and bounds, but it lacked control in spending," Susan said.

I didn't tell Susan my true opinion because I didn't want to hurt her feelings. I knew her well enough to know that she always had a problem with over-spending, even in her personal life. She had never taught herself to sacrifice for a goal. Susan was 75% emotions.

I felt like telling her, "Susan, I find excuses extremely offensive, boring, and irritating. I don't believe in them!"

Instead, I told her, "Your excuse sounds very logical.

The only problem is, it won't stand a chance in the court of success!"

It is essential, especially during times when your company lacks manpower, that a business owner use his or her supply of energy intelligently. You have to treat the source of your energy intelligently and distribute it wisely.

For myself, I believe that the source of our human energy is clean living. I stay away from nicotine, alcohol, and other drugs. I exercise and rest in concert with the rhythms of nature. In other words, I go to bed in time to rise with the sun. I firmly believe that is the first step toward maximizing the flow of energy during business hours.

Susan smoked. She didn't exercise. She was an emotional eater. She handled her personal finances poorly. She worked many hours, but she never got very much accomplished. When she stayed to work late on one day, the next day she always paid the price.

In short, Susan lived according to her emotions. Although she was intelligent, her emotions always won out. Since the majority of the population conducts their business during the early hours and at that time of day Susan was just barely hanging in there, it was no surprise to me that her business failed.

Living by your emotions is a dangerous situation for any business owner. Like any other weakness, it will only get worse with age.

The only way we stand a chance to get our portion of the delicious pie of success is if we manage to act with our intelligence instead of our emotions!

Several years back, Lotti arranged for a Frito-Lay sales meeting at the magnificent Inn of the Mountain God in Mescalero, New Mexico. Frito-Lay requested that Lotti supply a casket.

What did the management of Frito-Lay want with a casket? The leader of the meeting requested that the brands of all of their competitors be thrown in the casket. It was a very clever, demonstrative, and memorable idea.

I ended up calling a funeral home myself. The funeral director sounded like I hurt his feelings when I told him that no one had died. I couldn't get a casket. I ended up substituting the casket ritual with a high tea by the fire place.

I asked my staff to write down all the reasons why something cannot be done. I acted very sympathetic. Then, I demanded they tear up the piece of paper and throw it in the fireplace. The reasons were gone, and gone for good!

"So," I said, "this is a very historic moment in our company. From now on, we focus only on how to get things done. From this moment on, we will only talk positively. The office rent we are paying is too high for anything but positive talk.

"All of us will make every possible effort to sell the product our company wants us to sell. We will thoroughly educate ourselves about the benefits of these products. We must understand fully why we represent them and why the client will benefit from them.

"And, from now on, we will operate strictly by an award system. At the end of each month, every staff member will receive a computer printout to judge personal efforts. At the end of the year, our award system will recognize the winners."

Each member compiled another list. This one they kept because it contained only positive things. It listed all the benefits our firm preferred selling and it told why. Those staff members who did not attend the meeting were asked to copy the list in their own handwriting and mail it to me. I knew that hand writing something would help them remember the list. I wanted to make sure that everyone on the staff was thinking "positive," which would make them all less susceptible to "failure."

Motivation As The Key To Success

Whether we are students, parents, or teachers, salespeople, management, or civic leaders, in order to achieve maximum success for any motivation, we first have to:

a) Clearly define our goal.
b) Analyze and then establish what exactly motivates the people which are instrumental in assisting us in reaching the goal.
c) Inspire these people by providing them with an incentive, a goal, that appeals specifically to them.

This process has a proven success rate. It has worked for me and my business. And, it has the potential to work for anyone and any enterprise that is dependent upon the commitments and work excellence of other people, whether on a personal or professional level.

Telling a magazine a story about our adventure… and they paid for our lunch!

# CHAPTER 14

# TALKS WITH THE TOPS

*"Good judgement is based on experience.*
*Experience comes from bad judgement."*

I am truly impressed by people who, no matter what, are inspired to reach the top among their peers.

I used to ask myself, "How do they do it? What is their secret? Are they more brilliant then I am? What is their formula for success? How can I be successful like they are?"

"They" are the Top 50 American Express travel agents. Even though my travel agency has been counted among their number ever since American Express started this award program, I still learn from these people. And, you can, too!

These successful Top 50 people are at the pinnacle of their business and worthy of my interest and sometimes my imitation. In fact, we all, that is, all the Top 50 American Express travel agents, know the value of learning from each other. We know that success breeds success.

At business meetings, as I rub shoulders with them, I listen to their conversations. I notice that they enjoy each other's' company. They clan together. They exchange experiences and ideas, and they seem anxious to learn from each other. They talk productively and positively.

They use their time wisely even as they have fun at parties. It's apparent that they come to the meetings with a professional goal. They observe, and they listen.

They inspire.

Each autumn, when American Express releases the names of the year's Top 50 winners, I hurriedly read through all the names to see if

Envoye Travel made it and how we positioned ourselves. Envoye Travel has made the list every year since the program was initiated about 10 years ago. In 1989, we were 12th in the nation. I am still waiting for the 1990 figures.

In a sense, the recognition of being among the top winners is even more pleasing to my professional ego than any monetary supremacy.

When a travel agent asked me one time what it took to win, the first thing that came to my mind was: "You have to give it your absolute best."

Each year the Top 50 travel to an exotic destination somewhere in the world where they are wined and dined as special guests of American Express.

One of our Top 50 trips courtesy of American Express was to Hong Kong to celebrate our annual meeting. I was honored to be among them. That mild November day, the 50 of us with our companions cruised together across the South China Sea to the colorful Portuguese Island of Macau. The relaxed atmosphere on board the ship offered the opportunity I had been waiting for. I wanted to visit with several of the top achievers in the travel industry. The best souvenirs of a trip are the impressions one collects, and I was looking forward to taking home some new ideas with which to motivate my staff.

As I talked with the agents, I asked them what they did to become successful. The answers I gained that day ranged from common sense and innovation to dedication and determination.

All their secrets to success were amazingly easy. In fact, I was sure if I integrated their secrets into my agencies that by the next year my name would jump a few places ahead of my contenders!

And, Envoye Travel did jump a few places ahead the next year! What an inspiration for my staff!


Ivan Soler: The Personal Touch

I talked to Ivan Soler, one of my very favorite role models. The annual production of his Travel Network in Puerto Rico consistently places Ivan at the very top of the Top 50 list.

Curious, I asked Ivan what he thought he did that gave him an edge over his peers. Ivan seemed surprised as he shrugged his shoulders and said, "As an employer, I feel a sense of responsibility, not only toward the consumer and my staff, but also toward society as a whole, especially toward the so-called underdog. I am more motivated by helping others than by a long digit number in my bank account."

"My mission is to help and to inspire others, whether they are clients or whether they are people looking for a place to work. To provide people with the possibility to excel and to broaden their horizons by seeing the world - that is my motivation," he told me.

Then he told me something that is amazingly simple, sensible, and extremely beneficial to any travel agency owner. It could easily serve as monument to the importance of common sense in any industry.

When Ivan arrives at the office, he checks with his travel counselors to find out what travel requests came into the office while he was out. The major ones, in particular travel requests to foreign destinations, he follows up personally, by calling the client. In this manner, he has control of his sales.

Back in my own office in Lubbock, Texas, I adopted Ivan's technique right away. These days I don't have to ask my travel counselors about special travel requests that they have received. When I arrive at my office, I find notes already on my desk.

When I call the clients, I identify myself as owner and manager, and I thank them for the confidence they demonstrated toward my firm. I volunteer special travel tips.

I ask if they have any particular questions and assure them of my personal involvement in their travel arrangements which of course my travel counselor is handling for them. Many times that one call is all it takes to be awarded the client's business repeatedly.

Several of our clients have expressed amazement that I, as owner and manager, take the time and the personal interest in contacting them. I'm just following a proven path to the top, a path which anyone who intends to be a successful travel agency owner should follow: keeping the personal touch in my business.


Dan Dipert: The Value of Persistence

At another American Express meeting, one that took us to Club Med Don Miguel on Spain's Costa del Sol, I looked around the huge swimming pool for Dan Dipert, a very special person and owner of Dan Dipert's Travel which is headquartered in Arlington, Texas.

When I found Dan and congratulated him on being among the top of the Top 50, he said, "Sigrid, the money in travel is found at the "Senior Citizens Club" or whatever they might have christened their organization.

"Look for them in the yellow pages. Seniors have the time to travel. They have the money. And, they enjoy travel presentations."

It was later that night as all of us gathered on the terrace for a cocktail party when I saw Dan again. Dan confessed, "One of the first rules for success is to be persistent. Never give up. Believe me, in my past there were times, when I didn't know if I would ever see the light at the end of the tunnel. But, I hung in there and worked hard with absolutely nothing left but persistence. I took one step at the time until I finally won."

I could identify with Dan's experience. Loyalty to a goal is as important as loyalty to a friend.

Dan creates his own tours - Dan Dipert's Tours. But, he also selects certain tours already on the market. He combines both products and successfully markets them in his personalized, detailed brochure. The name Dan Dipert has become a very special attraction in the travel industry.


Vicky Kaplan: Success Takes Effort

My ears perked up during a recent meeting at the Harvey Hotel in Dallas. Vicky Kaplan, manager of Dan Dipert's Travel in Little Rock, Arkansas, in describing one of her "keys to success" gave me a new idea for increasing sales and confirmed my approach to the travel business: the opportunity for travel sales is everywhere if we just make the effort to recognize the opportunity!

"Delivering an airline ticket to a commercial client presents a tremendous sales opportunity," Vicky said.

"Hey," she told me, "those clients travel! When I deliver a ticket for a business trip, I deliver a vacation brochure as well. Why not? It doesn't take any extra time and the clients love it. I have picked up quite a bit of vacation business from commercial accounts that way."

"Effort," I thought. "Success takes effort, that extra amount of energy only winners are willing to spend."

I suddenly remembered the considerable amount of brochures we throw away at the beginning of each year. And, I pondered about all the inspiration they could have aroused among the staff of our commercial accounts.

I wondered how many lost opportunities to sell a vacation package each outdated brochure represented.

Here is a new opportunity for our agency: From now on, we will include a vacation brochure with every commercial ticket delivery!

## Luther Carle: Using Innovation

More recently, I jogged around the long spacious deck of the new Star Princess enjoying a Caribbean cruise. Luther Carle, a travel agent who was also attending the same American Express Top 50 meeting, joined me.

Luther Carle of Suburban Travel in Berlin, Connecticut, has the charisma of a typical winner. He used the time we walked together productively and launched into a most inspiring exchange of business ideas.

Luther is a great sports fan - a tennis enthusiast. One of his ambitions is to play tennis on different courts all around the world. He has found a successful way to combine his hobby with his work as a travel agent.

Every year he purchases an updated mailing list of members from different tennis clubs around the nation. Routinely and faithfully he targets these members with his tennis packages featuring tennis events and tennis clinics at different tennis resorts. I believe his tennis packages will become quite prestigious in time.

When I spoke with him on board the Star Princess, he had just returned from accompanying one of his groups to the Club Med property in Huatulco, Mexico, and was preparing to take another group to the Mediterranean and the Black Sea on board the Crown Princess.

## Martha and James Cross: The Finest Possible Service

When I attend the Top 50 meeting, I always look for familiar faces, someone I have become friends with over 18 years of patronizing meetings. Two of my favorite people are Martha and James Cross, owners of Arcadiana Travel in Lafayette, Louisiana.

Their success in the travel industry is closely tied to their constant efforts to provide the traveler with the finest possible service. In 1989,

Martha and James won the first prize for best service of the year. American Express invited them to New York City for a deluxe, all-expense-paid vacation and rewarded them $4,000 in traveler's checks.

What did Martha and James do that was so outstanding? James answered the phone at home late one night. An American Express Credit Card holder was stranded on her way through Lafayette. She had a flat tire and no money.

James crawled out of his bed, went to his office, got some Travelers Cheques, and delivered them to the woman. In no time at all, his client was back on the road again.

His efforts with his customers are worthy of the first place prize for service from American Express, and are worthy of imitation by anyone interested in being a successful travel agency owner.

The Last Word: There's No Free Ride!

These winners have no miracles to success, and they have no secrets. What they do have is a lot of common sense, a lot of dedication, professional pride, joy, enthusiasm, creativity, loyalty, and an eagerness to please the client coupled with the desire to be among the best.

My team has made the American Express Top 50 list every year. I attribute our achievement to the successful combination of characteristics I've discussed in this book, which may be summed up as follows:

* My staff is enthusiastic and well-informed.
* We are open for business until 9 p.m. at night and on weekends, when a majority of our competitors are closed.
* My firm has an incentive program that motivates success. It has the same philosophy as the free market economy - awards are given according to personal efforts.
* I occupy the front desk and can give my personal attention to any client who walks through our front door.
* I enjoy competition, and I give it all I have, never losing confidence that I am going to win.
* I am always open to learning new ideas and new techniques to improve our sales, our environment, and our attitudes.

This summary is only a brief overview of the ingredients to running a successful travel agency. Add it to your list for success.

Remember, there are no miracles to success, and there are no secrets. Just a lot of common sense, dedication, professional pride, joy, enthusiasm, creativity, loyalty, and an eagerness to please the client - coupled with the desire to be among the best!

If you wish to join us at a Top 50 American Express meeting in some exotic locale, then you have only to follow this proven formula for success. I hope to meet you there for an interesting exchange of ideas. I will look forward to learning from your experiences just as I have learned from others' experiences and just as you are learning from mine!

# CHAPTER 15

# AMERICAN EXPRESS ADVANTAGE

*"Alone we can do so little; together we can do so much."* –Helen Keller

In the travel industry, American Express enjoys the same prestige as Tiffany, Steuben Glass, and Mercedes-Benz. To the consumer, these names are all synonymous with high quality, integrity, and dependability. These names carry clout. They elicit the highest consumer expectations.

When choosing an American Express Travel Agency, a client expects more than mere hotel accommodations or an airline ticket. The client expects to be pampered.

From the beginning of the transaction all the way through to the very end, the client expects to be looked after in the best possible way by the most caring agents in the entire travel industry.

Why the American Express network?

There were many reasons, many American Express advantages that made me want to affiliate with the American Express network.

First, a deciding factor in my choice was the prestige and world-wide recognition of American Express. Whether in Qatar or Switzerland, South Dakota or North Carolina, there is an American Express Representative Office. People around the world know the name. They don't have to be told what it stands for.

Second, I am a perfectionist. I enjoy the challenge of executing a job to the consumer's highest expectations. I believe in excellence. The American Express network maintains these same standards. American

Express stands for excellence in the travel industry, and it is an honor to have my company associated with theirs.

American Express leadership in the travel industry was another unique quality which attracted me to the company. Leadership demands creativity, and American Express has provided it.

For example, American Express invented the traveler's check (or Travelers Cheques, as they spell it) and, eventually, the credit card.

Today's traveler may take these two innovations for granted, but they are two of the most important travelers' aids. The traveler's check and the credit card were the American Express Company's answer decades ago to the problems posed by traveling with cash, which was the only alternative at that time.

In those days, travelers crossing North America were frequently targets for gunmen in search of cash. The American Express Company responded to the challenge this problem presented by inventing traveler's checks which were worthless to thieves.

These handy personal checks could be purchased on one coast and cashed on the other. Robbing travelers, at least for reasons of obtaining cash, soon became a fruitless pursuit for the robber.

So you see, even from the beginning, the travel industry benefited greatly from the American Express Company's constant efforts to serve the public, to make travel safe and enjoyable.

You might be as surprised as I was when I first learned about the circumstances which led to those two inventions. Terrorism and robbery, which some of us perceive to be a modern evil, is as old as travel, and travel is as old as human beings. These evils led to the American Express invention of the traveler's check and, eventually, the credit card.

The third major traveler's aid pioneered by American Express was a world-wide network of travel agencies. When the first American Express Travel Agencies popped up around the world, they greatly simplified travel.

American Express tried to give the traveler the feeling of having a home away from home. The American Express Offices all over the world were friendly places where travelers were able to find travel assistance.

In these American Express agencies, travelers could make hotel reservations, receive worldwide assistance, pick up messages and mail, purchase Travelers Cheques, cash personal checks, and buy tickets for steamship travel, tours, cruises, and airline transportation. For a traveler in trouble, these offices were as welcome a sight as the American flag at a consulate or embassy.

While three of our clients were in Paris one year, the U.S. dollar suddenly plunged to a dramatic low. Shops and restaurants, even hotels, stopped accepting the U.S. dollar overnight. There was a massive panic everywhere.

Tourists were stranded - except those seasoned travelers who had the sense to travel with American Express Travelers Cheques. In Paris, U.S. tourists stood in long lines in front of the American Express Office to change their dollars into Travelers Cheques.

American Express stood firmly behind their commitment. Merchants knew they would get their money.

"If it had not been for American Express," one of the ladies told us, "we really would have been up a creek. Let me tell you, we were very impressed."

Some of these American Express original travel aids snowballed into incredible successes. Consequently, they have inspired many derivatives. But, none of the imitators can equal American Express, the original.

The immediate benefit of being part of a major travel network is instant customer recognition. Customer recognition is particularly important in a society like ours, whose members are extremely mobile.

Also, for a small or new business, bonding to a major network can make the difference between success and failure, especially when you consider that the network's name lends its reputation and credibility to the name of the agency in the eyes of the customer.

Instant recognition by travelers was not the only major benefit my company experienced through my alliance. My company's advertising opportunities were greatly enhanced. The American Express logo that accompanied my products proved of great value as it encouraged confidence among my customers.

In today's business climate, mass media advertising (TV, radio, and newspaper commercials) is very expensive, and, in many cases, it is unaffordable. The small business with an alliance to a major network gains exposure in the local market through the network's national advertising campaigns.

The American Express logo also helps me when I place my Sunday newspaper advertisement in the travel section. Some of my clients confide to me that they always look for the American Express logo first. They enjoy the American Express reminder: Why take a chance when you take a trip? I think that says it all. I place it in my Yellow Page ad each year, too.

Sherry, one of my travel counselors, was on cloud nine recently thanks to a phone call soliciting her assistance for travel arrangements by a large group flying to Venezuela. The caller lived in Amarillo, a town with several travel agencies and a full 90 miles north of our office in Lubbock. The client called our firm because we were an American Express Representative Office.

In addition to the instant recognition and free exposure to national advertising campaigns, my travel agency earns higher commissions by virtue of being a member of an international network.

Rather than the normal 10 percent commission a travel agency retains after the sale of a product, as a member of the network, the travel agency now receives considerably higher commissions. Because the collective sales of the entire conglomerate are naturally higher than the sales of an individual travel agency, suppliers, such as cruise lines, tour operators, hotels, and car rental companies, award us a considerably higher commission scale as members of a network.

I am always proud to hand someone my business card with the American Express logo on it. In many cases it gives me the extra edge over the "Generic Travel Agency."

What can I say? I am one of those people who is very proud to be a member of the American Express family. In return, I give it my loyalty. I am always proud to introduce American Express products to my clients.

"There is no greater travel value for the price," I remind my co-workers and my clients.

In brief, the many advantages of being affiliated with the American Express network may be summarized as follows:

1. Prestige and customer recognition.
2. Credibility with clients and throughout the travel industry.
3. Leadership through excellence, creativity, and innovation.
4. Enhanced advertising opportunities.

American Express is the travel network that is most widely known, the most prestigious, and has the longest track record in the travel industry. American Express met all my business needs, and it gave my company an important edge over local competitors.

Joining the American Express Network

When I started my own travel agency in 1971, I soon realized the importance of the American Express clout and the services the company offers. I eagerly pursued an alliance between American Express and my travel agency.

American Express appoints only one agency in a given area. A major local competitor of mine had already applied to be the American Express representative in our area. An evaluation period between my competitor and my company began, monitored by American Express. It ended in my victory. I believe the reason why American Express selected my agency was because of my product knowledge, work ethics, and long working hours.

I was following good business instinct when I sought a relationship with American Express. And, I intended it to be my sole affiliation as far as networks were concerned because I am a firm believer that, in business as in marriage, one can only enjoy a successful alliance with a single partner.

I have always had an instinct for quality. At one time, I worked for Tiffany's in New York City; I recognized the quality and beauty of Steuben Glass; and, at the time, I drove a Mercedes-Benz! Therefore, the American Express connection was, for me, a natural choice over any other network.

I was extremely proud when Gene Willis and I finally signed the contract that tied my bond with American Express. I wish to commemorate Gene who died of a heart attack on the busy streets of New York City. Gene was one of the finest American Express executives I ever met.

I shall always cherish my memory of the first day I hung the sign saying "American Express Office" over my front entrance, and when, for the very first time, I answered the phone, "Thank you for calling Envoye Travel/American Express."

Of course, when Gene and I signed that first contract, I did not understand the full implications of the advantages of being affiliated with the American Express network. Today, after a nearly 20-year-old association between American Express and my company, I can clearly say that I have highly benefitted from our marriage.

I sincerely hope American Express has found in me the loyalty it deserves as a partner who upholds its very high business standards.

Using American Express Standards Throughout Your Agency

The American Express standards reflect my own business philosophy as well. Their pledge to serve the public always comes first, and I believe this to be true. Conducting business according to these high standards is the only way I can feel good about myself and enjoy my job.

Whether it is only one member of your staff or the entire agency, it is vital that the professional values and the office performance align with the standards of the network they represent. In my agencies, I see to it that we reflect the high standards of the American Express network.

Additionally, in our office, all of the travel counselors enthusiastically introduce our clients to travel products from suppliers who have the status: "Preferred by American Express." The preferred status guarantees quality and financial responsibility.

In the event a supplier goes out of business, American Express covers any possible losses the client or the travel agent might have suffered. This is another example of the excellence to which American Express adheres, where serving the public comes first.

Whenever a chance presents itself, I try to point out to my agents the advantages of being an American Express representative office and how our association with a major network helps them and the office.

When we serve the public, we serve ourselves. The fringe benefits from such a commitment are incredible. Voila! At the end of the year, the numbers in my firm's bank account are in the black - and higher than expected. The agents in my office have benefitted from increased sales, and we have all benefitted from the repeat customers who are impressed by the services we provide.

I try to enhance the awareness of my agents of the many American Express Special Services which include Travelers' aids like Travelers Cheques sales and refunds, Gift Cheques, and Travel Protection Plans. All of these draw additional travelers into our offices, travelers who otherwise might never have found us or paid any attention to us.

* Ursula, in our financial department, assisted a client with the sale of English Pound American Express Travelers Cheques. The client was a group leader who regularly escorted a tour to Europe. Because of Ursula's efficient service and her efforts to solicit the client's business as well as the convenience to the client of conducting all the details of the trip at

one location, the client came to us for arrangements of the group trip the following year.

\* A traveler visiting Lubbock lost his wallet. His American Express Credit Card, Travelers Cheques, airline ticket - everything was gone. From the friend's house where the traveler was spending the weekend, he called the American Express toll-free number and was referred to our firm. When he arrived in our office two hours later, we replaced his credit card, Travelers Cheques, and airline ticket.

The host family he visited were so impressed that the family decided to travel with us. The head of the family managed a large firm, and we received that business as well.

\* We got a another big account the other day thanks to Rita's excellent service and because we offer Travelers Aids Services. The leader of a church group which travels to Switzerland each spring visited the office only to discuss the matter of getting a supplementary card for one of the students traveling with the group.

Rita gave the gentleman excellent service and reminded him of all the other ways we could assist him with his trip: hotel and air reservations, transfers in Switzerland, and even setting up concerts and sightseeing trips. He liked the idea of conducting business with a one-stop travel agency. Because we could offer these services, we added another pleased client to our growing list.

Excellence Through Total Service

Our company motto is: We want to make travel as pleasant and as easy as possible. Therefore, in addition to the American Express services, we take passport pictures, assist with visas and passport information, and deliver tickets and itineraries.

These services augment the American Express services and allow us to offer our customers total service. Total service is our standard, and the American Express standard.

Whenever we send a client to a foreign country, our travel counselors recommend that our firm makes special business or sightseeing arrangements ahead of time. It's a great help to the client and an easy procedure for our counselors.

All my firm has to do is to phone or fax the representative office in the city the client will be visiting and relay the wishes of our client. We are only able to offer this service through the American Express network.

Frequently, when we send a client abroad, we contact the American Express Representative Office in a town in which the client will spend a few days and make special arrangements through the local Representative Office.

We talk to an agent we know and have met at an American Express meeting. It helps in getting the best assistance available. For example, two history-oriented clients decided to attend Octoberfest in Munich last fall. Rather than letting them struggle for themselves and miss out on a very important part of German history, I asked my friend at the American Express Office in Munich to provide them with the best possible guide.

In their own words, the Thomas's had the time of their lives because their guide Peter brought the history of the famous Octoberfest to life for them. Peter gave them the real story of Octoberfest, about the folk festival celebrated by all the people who wanted to show their appreciation to their ruler for not charging them any taxes.

Mr. and Mrs. Thomas enjoyed their visit so much so, that following year they inspired the congregation of their Baptist church to travel to, of all places, the Octoberfest in Munich.

We were enthusiastic about their business and their trips. I reserved the dining room for them in the Vier Jahreszeiten Hotel which has large windows facing the Maximillian Strasse. That gorgeous room had an excellent view, by the way, of the colorful parade which, on Saturday morning, marches past the hotel on its way to the Wiesen where the festival officially opens.

I will also call my friend at the American Express in Munich and request Peter, the super guide, to narrate the parade and to explain to my clients all the wonderful traditions displayed and the fabulous costumes worn by the men and women walking and dancing in the parade. Many of these colorful costumes are several hundred years old. Some are extremely valuable museum pieces, family heirlooms passed on traditionally to the oldest boy or girl of a family.

The Octoberfest parade is fun just to look at, but to those spectators given the opportunity to learn its history, it rises in stature, from being a colorful amusement to an unforgettable, historical event!

Upon his return, Mr. Thomas told me, "Sigrid, just imagine, we were seated at the Octoberfest in the stall normally reserved for the

Oberburgermeister (the mayor) of Munich. And, did you know Peter was the personal guide for President Carter in Munich?"

I have even gone so far as to board my client's dogs. However, I don't recommend this particular service to other agencies. Dogs are not like people. They bite.

Last week we had a major crisis in our Envoye West Office. A client's teenage son had just flown to Sao Paulo, Brazil, to spend a year as an exchange student. Upon arrival in Sao Paulo, the son could not produce the visa required by law in order to stay in Brazil as a student. The airline planned to deport him back to the United States. The son placed a frantic call to his father. The father called Dolores, his travel agent and my office manager. Only briefly was there panic all the way around.

"Wait a minute," Dolores said as she calmed the client down. "If I remember correctly you paid for your son's airline ticket with your American Express Credit Card, so we are in good shape."

Delores called American Express Global Assistance, and they immediately started to work on the problem. "Global Assistance was absolutely wonderful," Dolores raved to me later. "They could not do enough!"

"They sent a special representative to the airport who prevented the deportation of the young man," Delores continued.

"The representative had the local authority to issue the necessary permit immediately.

"Not only did they manage for the son to stay in Brazil, which I thought was a miracle in itself, but after everything was taken care of, they called the father here in Lubbock and then they even called me to report that the crisis had been resolved."

The father was so impressed that he came by the office to rave about American Express. He said he would tell all his buddies on the golf course how American Express has helped him in a real crisis.

He swore he would keep his American Express credit card for as long as he lived and have American Express take care of all his travel needs from now on.

The father was not kidding. The next morning, his secretary called to switch all of the company's commercial travel over to our travel agency.

"Incredible...," I thought, "how one person's good service can snowball into a major benefit for an entire company."

Here I am, a travel agent in West Texas and because of a colleague of mine in Sao Paulo, Brazil, performing an excellent job, I benefit. What a great example of how this distinguished network works!

Personal Advantages of Being An American Express Representative

Not only does our affiliation with the American Express network help all of us from a business and financial standpoint, but also there are personal advantages to being a part of the network for all employees.

Take the American Express Health insurance plan. There is not a better one on the market. In fact, some of my co-workers, who are presently insured through their spouses, after taking a look at the American Express insurance plan, have told me they will be switching over.

Other personal advantages in association with American Express are more obvious. Consider one of my latest experiences:

I was in Hamburg waiting in a long line to check in at the hotel. The woman in front of me was also a travel agent. When she got to the receptionist, she wanted the same thing I wanted: a magnificent room with a view across the Alster, at a 50 percent travel agency discount!

The clerk apologized but said that it would be impossible to comply with her request because there was a large convention in the hotel. The travel agent understood and accepted a standard room at a public rate. Then, it was my turn. Same scenario, except that the desk clerk looked at my business card.

"Ah, you are with American Express! They give us," she told me, "a lot of business each year. Their groups stay in our hotel."

I did not push the issue about the travel agency discount. The poor hotel had to make a profit, too. Right? I expected a standard room at public rates.

When I checked into my room, I was stunned. The room was gorgeous complete with a view of the famous Alster, the waterway which connects the center of the city to the North Sea.

My phone rang. The desk clerk was checking to see if I was satisfied with my room. "It's a great room. I love it," I said. "Pardon me, but, how much is it?" "With the 50 percent travel agency discount rate, it comes to...let's see here..."

"That's fine. Thank you very much," I said looking across a beautiful part of my homeland. I thought, "What a wonderful world. The world of a travel agent - of an American Express travel agent."

Another very important personal advantage of being a member of the American Express family is the opportunity for professional growth. Managing a business puts a heavy demand on my time. Consequently, I am very selective about which travel industry meetings I attend.

I cannot think of one American Express meeting I have missed since my appointment. The American Express meetings are not only very educational. With the high-caliber travel agents one meets and exchanges ideas with, these meetings are also extremely inspiring and motivating.

The American Express Seminars are also top-notch. They are held in different cities around the country and are the best in the travel industry.

The American Express Pledge: Service to the Public

In all my years with American Express, I cannot recall one instance in which American Express failed to follow through on their commitment to the customer.

During an annual American Express meeting, an agent from the American Express representative office in Midland, Texas, stood up and told us that American Express does a lot of things we never hear about.

"Remember a while back, when a little girl fell into an abandoned well shaft in Midland?" she asked the assemblage. "The national news covered little Jessica's plight and her rescue. What we didn't hear about on the national news was that American Express gave the rescue efforts carte blanche. Without American Express' authorization," she continued, "the rescue efforts to save Jessica would have been hampered by devastating time delays."

On the humorous side to all but the woman involved, our firm assisted an American Express Credit Card holder who ended up in jail for driving a rental car while holding only an expired drivers license and her American Express Card.

The driver was from out of town and did not have access to any cash to pay the jail bond. While in jail, she was allowed to place one telephone call. She called American Express.

That same afternoon, one of my counselors went to the jail with Travelers Cheques, satisfying the judge, and the woman was freed.

You will find other examples throughout this book of how service-minded American Express, Envoye Travel, and all the affiliated members are. Remember the agent who voluntarily left his bed to deliver Travelers Cheques to a stranded American Express card holder?

Nothing could be a better proof of the American Express commitment of servicing the consumer than the actions of its network members. That agent won the American Express grand prize for the most outstanding service which included, in addition to a large cash prize, a first-class trip to New York City, all expenses paid. The American Express Company sets an example with their incentives as well as their business standards.


The Final Word

It's stimulating to belong to the American Express Network, to say the least! And, now you know how a travel agent, an American Express travel agent, can make a difference to you, your travel agency, and your customers. Now you know why being in the American Express network can make you so much more than just another travel agent!

Of course, anyone can make a mistake. Underneath everything, American Express is only human, too. Occasionally they do make mistakes, just like you and I do. However, when a mistake is made, American Express does not relax their standards or their ethics. It's nice to know they always make up for it, usually in more than one way - because the American Express goal is to please the client!

The American Express goal is to please the client. That is my goal and my way of doing business and approaching life in general, too. If I make a mistake, I admit it, and I want to make up for it. It's my way of staying pleased with life.

It's also a way of sleeping well at night, of enjoying sunrises, of feeling good in your heart, and of being able to commune with nature and all the wonders of the world. It's a way to remain soft and sensitive and tender inside your heart, so none of the beauty around you escapes your senses.

Ultimately, there is nothing more important than pleasing others. Can you think of one single thing that makes traveling through life more of an adventure?

I like to think that every one of my co-workers is as proud of our prestigious marriage to the American Express Company as I am - and as loyal. Every person in our office fully realizes that the client, particularly the new client, comes to our company expecting the highest quality that the entire travel industry has to offer.

Put simply, to the clients, we are American Express. We are American Express first, not Judy or Marie or Robert. Eventually, by proving ourselves, we become Judy or Marie or Robert to our clients. We are proud to provide service befitting the most service-minded peers in our industry. This is our daily challenge.

To summarize the key benefits of the American Express Network, what pops up first in my mind is:

* Instant name recognition
* Free national name advertising
* Highest quality of training for professionals
* Higher earnings
* No risk-taking in case of financial default by a preferred supplier
* Best health care for employees

To me, these benefits justify the annual membership fee. But, then, I am a realistic person who realizes that there is no such thing as a free lunch.

For me, being a member of the American Express family, means my efforts and loyalty are well rewarded.

# CHAPTER 16

# OUTSIDE SALES

*"The power of choice"*

Now that you know the fun game I play each day, the one that rewards me with the fringe benefit of traveling like a millionaire without being one, you might wish to follow in my footsteps and become a travel agent.

But, if personal circumstances prevent you, or someone you know, from subscribing to my religion, don't despair. There are some other very attractive options for traveling like a millionaire without being one, options that, if properly used, will add to the travel agency's sales.

You would be amazed at what a motivated person can do to help themselves travel like a millionaire without being one, even on a part-time basis. You might even discover how easy it can be and how much fun investing some of your energy so that the dividend for a friend or outside sales associate is seeing the world in grand style, without having to pay Onassis prices.

Here is how a travel agent can increase sales through motivated individuals outside the agency. Sometimes this involves sharing a part of the agency profits with outside sales persons. Other times, this approach only involves a little creative planning on the part of the agent.

Either way, it is important to remember that you would not normally have access to these sales and they make an excellent supplement to your regular sales. I see this kind of situation much like I see being a travel agent: Where other people have to deal with win-lose or lose-lose situations, this is a win-win situation!

Who to Approach

The majority of outside sales agents in our firm hold other jobs as well. They are attracted to the outside sales position by the benefits the travel industry offers such as free or reduced travel and extra income.

Let's face it, in today's world, if a sales person makes a sales call, it can be valuable to represent several product lines on one call.

Additional benefits for the outside sales person are flexible working hours and being able to target a specific market. For instance, an outside sales person is in a perfect position to inspire group travel.

Since the outside sales agent has few obligations inside the office, he or she exercises a much greater control over specific sales. An outside sales person can reach an agreement with a travel agent that he or she wants to represent. And, simply by referring clients to the agency, they can receive a referral fee.

A frequent flyer, like the man I told you about in the introduction, can usually make his own deal for the lowest and best prices. Yet, even frequent travelers can add to your outside sales because, just like other motivated people, they would like to travel first class all the time.

But, what about the motivated individuals who are not frequent flyers, who do not have a company paying the way or who only have two weeks for vacation? You can help them and help yourself at the same time.

Before you start, remember that I keep saying "motivated" individuals. It is my belief that you cannot motivate lazy or uninspired people. Don't waste your time looking for outside people who might not be motivated.

The right people, driven people, will find you. These people are motivated, but they probably will not have your expertise or imagination. It can only benefit you if you are ready for them with an offer, or a deal, that will work for them and for you.


The Options You Have

For people who have access to the public, like an insurance executive or a nurse, there are vacation and cruise discount coupons that can be distributed. When a certain number of those packages are sold, the person may qualify for the same vacation package or cruise or an airline ticket free, just as you or one of your agents might qualify.

For people who are members of an organization or just have a group of friends who want to travel, it is a mathematical solution. They can sell as little as four tickets or tours and go free themselves by dividing the total cost by one less passenger. This is known in the travel industry as the "1-free-4." For most cruises, the "1-free-15" is the standard. The organizer goes free. And, in some cases, there are additional volume discounts available to all the participants.

For people who do not have a group of friends or an organization of people who want to travel, there are other deals available. For example, a student, who might not have access to a group of people who can afford the cost and the time to travel, would still have access to other students flying home for the holidays.

By offering to pick up and deliver the tickets, by helping the students with scheduling, even by offering to share a part of the profits...by any or all of these marketing techniques, a motivated student would be able to make enough to pay for their own ticket home because they have access to volume ticket sales. The travel agency makes 10% on their sales. You can share 1/3 or 1/2 of this profit with the refreshed, motivated student who has brought you all this business.

These examples are only a few of the many ways you and your agency can work with outside people. Your imagination is the key to creating an atmosphere where the motivated individual and the agency both profit!


What You Tell the Motivated Person

"The time to start your planning is NOW. It's later than you think."

Remember my story about the lemons in the beginning of this book? I treasured the lemons until they had spoiled and it was too late to use them. You must explain this attitude to your motivated would-be traveler. Here is an example of the approach that has worked for me:

"Enact your dream right now. If you postpone your dream, you will never do it: 85% of the things we postpone, we will never do.

And, you must remember that anything worth having is worth working for. If traveling like a millionaire was easy, then everyone would be in first class. You can do it, but you must be willing to spend the time it takes to research, to plan, and to work toward your goal as you will see in the examples below.

Keep your goal in mind. Replenish your energy every morning. Look in the mirror and tell yourself there is absolutely no reason why you should continue to live without the same advantages that other people have:

'Why can't I see the world?'

'What is it like to stay in the luxurious hotel across the street from my economy accommodations?'

'Why can't I fly first class and get the royal treatment?'

Well, my friend, you can do it! Start by making a list of your priorities, and then make a list of people - anyone who travels."

Remind the motivated individual that there is no free lunch, no free ride. They will have to invest some time and energy into their new project. It takes time to plan a strategy, time to make reservations, advance time to get the best travel deals. But, the investment will be worth it when they are traveling like millionaires.

If you have some people who are motivated to do outside sales, but just cannot seem to get the right plan together for their particular situation, you can refer to them to the How to Travel Like a Millionaire Without Being One series: There is one designed for all people who want to travel like a millionaire without being one and one designed especially for senior citizens.


Meet a Few Friends Who Travel Like Millionaires

As you will see, there are many fascinating individuals who travel like millionaires without being one. These are some of the people I have met over the years while I lunched in first class on planes, jetting around the world exploring different corners of our amazing planet. I think these people will impress you.

If you read the introduction, you have already met Barbara and Steve seated with me up in first class. Now meet a few of my other first class world-travelers and find out what they do in order to travel in the style of the rich and famous. Meet: Tina, the nurse; David, the writer/artist; Pam, the school teacher; and Peter, the insurance salesperson.

All of these people have several things in common. First, they all realize, there is no free lunch in life. Second, they all know that a positive attitude is an asset.

"If there where such a thing as a free lunch can you imagine how dull life would be?" Tina says.

Peter is equally outspoken about the richness that challenges add to life. According to Peter, a life without our daily personal Olympics, without our daily victories, no matter how small or how big they might seem to others, would be meaningless.

"The very fact, that we pay a price for everything we do and want, makes everything much more exciting, much more of a challenge, than being handed a 'free-bie.' It is the challenge that motivates us, that creates the energy to mold our life and ignites in us that warm feeling of pride. Paying a price is really something positive and gives value to our achievements.

"Plus, we can make it a parcel of fun. Much depends on our personal attitude. Let me tell you something about attitude that I heard recently at an American Express meeting in San Francisco:

A 7-foot-tall, 275-pound football player and a petite, 5-foot 2-inch tall, 102-pound cheerleader fly off for their honeymoon. In their hotel suite, the football player holds up his pants and says, 'Hoooney, see these big pants? Want to try them on? No? Good. And you better never try either. In our marriage, I am going to be the boss.'

The cheerleader smiles. She pulls her tiny nightgown from her travel bag. Holding it up, she says, 'Hoooney. See this tiny nightgown? Pretty, isn't it? Would you like to get into it? It's much too small? You can't get into it? Well, hoooney, you are right. And you will never get into it either...unless you change your damn attitude!'

Other characteristics my friends have in common are:

a) They enjoy their professions; b) They have lots of energy; c) They see themselves as first-class citizens who deserve the best; d) They are curious about the world and have the burning desire to experience as much as possible; and e) Of course, they want deluxe vacations, but only at budget prices.

Tina:
"My time is very important. In fact, as a nurse, I do not have much free time. Consequently, free time is precious. I am very selective about how I spend my free time away from my job.

"When I go on a vacation I enjoy staying in the best hotels. But I could never afford them until the day I shopped at Envoye Travel. That night at the travel agency's desk, I sighed over resort brochures with price tags for only the rich and famous. I confessed to the travel agent, I could not afford the vacation I really wanted. My friends, who usually travel with me could, but I couldn't.

"That's when the travel counselor told me I had three options. I could:

1) Organize a group and receive one free trip if 15 persons paid full price
2) Take the vacation I could afford.
3) Take the vacation I really wanted and pay for it - not with money, but with travel benefits I could accumulate during my free time. Free time? What free time?

"But then the travel agent insisted that I was sitting on an untapped gold mine. The travel agent was right. In my job, at the hospital, I was constantly surrounded by frequent travelers and those who could afford to travel but never did.

"The travel agent pointed out, that not only could I accumulate travel benefits at the hospital, but, just as important, I could bring "Stimmung" (an up-beat mood), into the hospital by inspiring people to see the world.

"I had nothing to lose by giving it a try. Instantly my remarks, like needing a reservation five years ahead of time for climbing Mount Everest and that I was taking deposits for the first commercial flight to outer space, caught everyone's imagination like a wild fire."

Tina became Miss Popular. In the lunch room, everyone raced to her table to sit with her. Rather than talking about work during her lunch break, she took a real break. She refreshed and re-energized her mind talking about Hawaii, Alaska. Europe, etc. Everyone perked up.

In Act II, Tina became more daring. She snuck a brochure of a Caribbean cruise on a patient's lunch tray. It was an historic event that marked the very first time for that particular patient to finish her meal.

Not only did the woman finish her meal in record time without realizing that she had inhaled the nutritious food, but she was so taken with the colorful pictures of St. Thomas, that Tina snuck her a video of a cruise. Three months later, that same patient was a smiling passenger om board the Royal Princess, cruising the Caribbean on her way to St. Thomas.

In a way, Tina made everyone a winner: The patient, her loved ones, her insurance company, the hospital, the cruise line, the travel agency, and Tina. In short, it is not farfetched to say that society as a whole benefitted from Tina's outside sales position as a travel agent.

At the hospital, many doctors and nurses as well as numerous patients have become Tina's clients. Her original hesitancy to let people at the hospital know about her moonlighting job soon disappeared. Tina's up-beat remarks about travel have made her a very popular nurse among patients and staff.

Now, when days are grey at the hospital, everyone turns to Tina for a morale-booster shot. She doesn't let anyone forget about the sunny side of life. Each day her enthusiasm brings the beauty of our planet into the rooms of the hospital.

Tina reminds every one of the fact that there is a whole wonderful world waiting for us, ready to be explored by those of us with the will to reach out for it.

Doctors don't have time to call a travel agency. Consequently many ask Tina to find out the best travel bargains.

Tina's attitude is particularly beneficial to those patients who think they have nothing to live for because they have nothing to look forward to.

It is a formidable thing to realize the power in a simple travel brochure. When Tina gives a patient a brochure of Hawaii or a cruise, the patient perks up. A trip gives them something desirable to anticipate. Tina calls it "my miracle cure." And, her patients refer to her as the nurse with the vital life charts, a.k.a. travel brochures.

Tina's patients are frequently on the road to recovery, and discovery, much sooner than the patients of other nurses.

Noticing this, some of the doctors have asked, "Tina, what's your secret.? Why are your patients a lot more positive than other patients?"

Tina tells them that it's because in the back of their minds is a trip to Hawaii.

If a patient tells her that he or she cannot afford to travel, Tina will prove to them that they can if they want to.

"Anybody can save a dollar a day," Tina tells them with a smile. "Just don't by that candy bar or that coke. If you save a dollar a day, you have

$365 at the end of the year. And, how does going to Acapulco for a few days sound to you?"

Making a person's dreams about travel seem closer perks up Tina's patients.

The phenomenal effect of travel on patients and the success of Tina's travel business, gave Tina the idea of putting a travel agency in the lobby of the hospital. She talked to the owner of the flower shop in the foyer of the hospital. The owner agreed. The beauty of a bouquet of flowers would be enhanced if it included a travel brochure. And, why not sell a travel gift certificate along with the flowers?

Tina offered the sales staff at the flower shop $5 for each travel gift certificate sold. That was at least as much as the shop earned on a bouquet of flowers. From past experience, Tina knew that a travel gift certificate would outshine flowers. After all, every patient would rather get a gift certificate toward a trip than flowers? A trip gets a person's hope for life rolling. And flowers? Well, they are very pretty, but they don't create the energy that the prospect of travel does.

Tina remembered when she broke her leg due to a ski accident and consequently was a patient in a hospital.

"When I woke up after my operation," Tina recalled, "all the flowers on my bedside table and the plants in my room they reminded me of a funeral. Yes, when I first opened my eyes back in my room after the operation, I felt like I was lying in a morgue. How nice a travel gift certificate would have been."

There were three major motives Tina considered that led her to Act III: 1) The positive effect travel had on Tina's surroundings; 2) Her income had risen; 3) She loved her profession as a nurse with an even greater passion than before because she had become more effective in healing patients.

The travel gift certificate idea inspired Tina to risk a giant step forward. She purchased a permit from the hospital administration to place an automated travel gift certificate dispenser in the lobby of the hospital. Soon, Tina intends to approach hospitals nationwide.

Tina vows that she will always want to be a nurse first, but, with a twinkle in her eye, she jokingly adds, "Besides, now that I am a moonlighting travel agent, I could not afford to resign from my job as a nurse. The hospital gives me too much business."

Tina's husband chuckled when she collaborated with him about the idea. He said, "Before you know it, you will be hiring an assistants to help you with all the vacation bookings you will receive, or you might even get into the automatic dispenser business." And, that is how Act III started.

"Well," Tina laughed, "Why not? You only live once!" According to Tina, the more you do, the more experiences you have. In the end, life is but a bundle of experiences. And the more you accomplish, the more your life is worth living.

My school teacher Herr Frieden in Germany once stood in front of our class and told the student next to me, "Hier schlaft Herr Junge weiter. Er war geboren und er starb." Here Mr. Junge continues to sleep. He was born and he died."

I vouched then, that this was not going to happen to me. Life was too short not to get the most out of it. Tina is right and it won't happen to her either. Her dual success first as a nurse and then as a travel agent give her the fringe benefit of seeing the world in the grandest possible style without having to pay Onassis prices. As Tina says, "I am a doer, not a viewer,"


David:


David is a writer. I met him for the very first time on an Air India flight, jetting from Delhi to Teheran. We both were traveling in the first class section of the Boeing 747.

Sitting next to each other feasting on caviar and vodka, it was only natural that our pleasure over the exquisite food should be enhanced by an exchange of thoughts with the stranger beside us.

"It's nice to fly first class." David whispered, mischief sparkling in his eyes. Leaning in my direction, he held a large white linen dinner napkin over his mouth to cover his whisper.

"It's nice indeed," I whispered back, "Especially in my case. I am not paying."

"You are kidding. I didn't pay either." David confided, "If you tell me your secret, I'll tell you mine!"

I confessed to him, "I am a travel agent."

"Well, I am a writer. I mentioned in my literature Air India, and, voila, I received a free ticket," David told me.

"It's amazing what you get just for the asking. In the early 60s, I worked on Oahu in Hawaii as a sales clerk. The Sheraton Hotel on

Maui had just opened. It was the first hotel on Kaanapali Beach. It was beautiful, and everyone in the Islands was talking about it. I had to see it.

"When I did go to see it, I fell in love with it. Its rooms were even decorated individually to please each customer's preference.

"The hotel was built over a mass of black lava rocks. In the 60s, it was the only hotel on a long, white expanse of beach. To the left of the hotel, the beach is warm and gentle. You walk to the right around the point of the lava rocks, and you cool down rapidly in the brisque wind of the North Pacific.

"I wanted to stay or to return and write my book in the hotel's inspiring environment. But my meager salary as a salesclerk restricted my stay to one night. One night only. "So I wrote a letter to the President of the Sheraton Corporation suggesting that I would stage the plot of my book in their hotel on Maui if, in exchange, he would allow me to stay for a certain time at a good price. Guess what? I received a yes from the president.

"Now, I am staying free at the Teheran Hilton. I used the same approach," David said as he raised his glass to me.


Pam:

On another trip, I spotted Pam two rows in front of me as our Alaska Airline flight made its final approach at the Juneau airport. I had never met her, but the very instant I saw her I knew that she was going to be part of our expedition which was going to assemble at the pier where the ferry bound for Haines docks loaded.

When I glanced at Pam I thought to myself, "Who would fly first class, wear a turtleneck sweater with moth holes in it, and carry an old, worn-out and shaggy raccoon coat whose mothball odor smelled offensively throughout the entire cabin of the plane - if not a member of our expedition.

My intuition was correct. Pam was my roommate in a small tent which perched on a different shore each night. During the day, we shared the ice-cold bottom of a rubber raft on the Tatenshini River. One night, while we were defrosting our feet by the camp fire, Pam told me how she had qualified for a substantial reduction of the cost of our exotic river expedition.

Pam was a school teacher with a most enticing history of inspiring students to travel. Just like in the case of Tina, where the hospital benefitted from the nurse-travel-agent, so Pam's school benefitted enormously from Pat the teacher-travel agent.

Pam had a certain talent for not only solving problems, but for turning problems into benefits. As a teacher, she combined the problems of today's students with her idea that a reward system is more enticing to the students than a system of punishment. So, Pam informed her students that those with the lowest number of days absent from class who were also willing to take a voluntary test proving them drug free would be taken free of charge on a senior trip.

To finance her project, she approached those merchants in her town which she traded with and requested assistance in helping finance the senior trip for the five winners.

"What you can do to make our town crime free" was the approach Pam used with the merchants.

While we were bouncing around in our rubber raft with the swift current of the Tatenshini River and nearly freezing to death, Pam's thoughts were in the sunny Caribbean.

"My next senior trip will be a Caribbean Cruise," Pam yelled across the thundering sound of the waves washing against our raft.

"The cruise line offers a free trip for every 16th passenger paying for accommodations in a 2-berth cabin. That means two seniors and I can travel free," she explained.

"Which senior students get to travel free?" I asked.

"The winners. The ones with the highest school attendance record, plus the hair sample proving them to be drug free."

I was impressed. Pam the teacher-travel agent was effectively fighting the problems of school absences and drug abuse at the same time.

Going one step further as a travel agent, Pam had also discovered a way of saving the local school district huge amounts of money. Pam had noticed that the teachers at her school and at the schools in surrounding districts paid high dollar prices for their airline tickets whenever they flew to an out of town teachers meeting.

The school boards traditionally authorized airline tickets that had no restrictions, but that privileged attached high-value price tags to the tickets. Pam, the furious taxpayer and creative travel agent who hated to see her tax dollars spent so ineffectively, introduced a plan that still allowed freedom for the traveler, yet cost the taxpayers considerably less.

Pam's plan was based on a flight-insurance policy that covered monetary loses of an airline ticket in the event of an emergency cancelation by a traveler.

Needless to say. Pam's reputation and success as a teacher-travel agent grew rapidly. Her victories in inspiring group travel made her an attractive target for tour operators, cruise lines, and airlines. On her desk invitations often piled up to participate in travel agency familiarization trips.

Peter:

Peter is the most successful insurance salesman in his town. He didn't have time to come to my office to make his vacation arrangements. So I volunteered to visit his office. I was impressed. In one corner of his office stood a round table which his secretary quickly converted into a dining table by placing a tablecloth over it. The business persons' lunch club on the top floor of the office building delivered our lunch, which the secretary had called in.

"Who wouldn't be impressed?" I immediately wondered, "If Peter is such a successful insurance representative, and he obviously is very creative, just look at the table, than he probably would be a heck of a good outside travel representative." I knew Peter was very popular with a lot of important persons in our area, people who travel a lot.

Other characteristics about Peter were: 1) He was an entrepreneur and motivated; 2) He was a very conservative spender, squeezing the maximum out of each dollar. When Peter traveled it was no frills all the way...unless someone else footed the bill.

Peter's eyes sparkled when I told him about staying at the Regent Hotel in Hong Kong recently, where my corner suite had a private terrace overlooking the South China Sea. And, that I arranged for an intimate reception around my private pool on my private lanai. I didn't forget to mention that my guests feasted on superb Chinese food which we ate with chopsticks carved out of real jade. And, I didn't forget to mention that Princess Dianna had stayed in the same suite or that the Duke of Edenborough during his visits to Hong Kong usually dines at the hotel's French restaurant.

I went into details about how the tables in the four- star restaurants were situated by the large picture windows facing the South China Sea which was dotted with interesting junks loaded with goods for Shanghai. Dining at the restaurant in general created the atmosphere of being on a cruise ship, I told him.

"That's how close the hotel is built to the edge of the South China Sea," I said.

Peter's imagination feasted on my words. I realized he was hooked and I took advantage of him - for both our sakes! I capitalized on Peter's passion for prestige and his love of traveling in the grand style.

I offered Peter my lifestyle. In exchange, he would sell travel to his famous clients through my travel agency. He did not have to move a finger. All he had to do was instruct his secretary to include with a customer appreciation certificate with his traditional New Year's card. The certificate would entitle the receiver to a discount on any 7-day cruise or escorted tour purchase at Envoye Travel. The gift certificate did not cost Peter a dime. Envoye Travel, in cooperation with the cruise lines and tour operators, supplied the gift certificates.

Like everything else, this was a game of productivity. If enough of Peter's clients booked, Peter and his wife, and maybe even his secretary, would travel free and in the grand style.

Peter was excited. His secretary was excited. She hurried to get the travel certificates in the mail as fast as possible. Peter's clients appreciated his thoughtfulness and recommended his insurance company to their friends.

And, Envoye Travel? They won a top sales award from Carnival Cruise lines and American Express.


A Reminder

Always remember that the opportunity for success is there for the motivated person. Whether you are a travel agent, an agency owner, or simply a traveler who wants to travel like a millionaire, anyone can succeed in their desires with time and a good attitude.

The most qualified people for outside sales are people who are already successful in other jobs or sales positions. These are the people with the necessary communications skills. They sometimes have a life that includes social exposure, but they also can be stay-at-home homemakers.

School teachers, nurses, sales persons, homemakers, students, or a leader at the senior citizens' club. All are excellent prospects for outside sales positions.

Remember, anyone can be successful at outside sales for your agency if they are motivated. You can guide them yourself or you can do them (and yourself) a favor by recommending the How to Travel Like a Millionaire Without Being One series for their specific needs: There is one for all people interested in traveling like a millionaire without being one and one especially for senior citizens.

Don't just look for motivated people to work in your agency or outside your agency, you must be motivated yourself to make it work!

# CHAPTER 17

# EASY STEPS FOR SUCCESS

*"The future belongs to those who believe in the beauty of their dreams."* –Eleanor Roosevelt

Anyone can succeed in the travel business, part-time or full-time, and reap the benefits of being a professional travel agent, provided they are a productive member of the industry.

In the beginning you must have a dream. A dream so powerful it keeps you awake at night. Don't delay your harvest by delaying your action. Launch your dream today, and become a successful travel agent.

Step 1:

Be desirable. To get your foot in the door of your new career and to get some first-hand knowledge about the true character of the travel industry, contact a travel agency in your area and volunteer to do an internship for a specific time period.

Agree on hours that are mutually beneficial. It probably will be best if you continue your present job until the time you are certain a career change is what you want.

For those who are not ready to quit their present job, part-time agents earn extra money and receive the same benefits as full-time agents. A part-time agent can pick up many clients through his or her full-time job.

During your job interview with a travel agency, make certain you point out how the agency will benefit through you. For example, convince the interviewer that you are willing to do all the leg work for the agents, including personalizing brochures with the travel agency's name, and filing brochures in designated places.

Make sure the interviewer knows that you will bring in new business - such as the travel arrangements for your friends, relatives, and, for those who have another job, business associates.

If you can get these points across, the chances for you to be accepted are almost certain. You might also work out an arrangement with a specific agent to do leg work in exchange for some computer instructions and general training.

Attending a travel agency school, especially one with an emphasis on computer training, is very helpful.

Note: There are labor laws that more often than not interfere with a person's incentives. In order to protect the agency from any labor violations, seek a written permission from the employment commission and the labor commission to make certain that no laws are broken.


Step 2:


Your success in the travel industry will greatly depend on your ability to market yourself and to market your product. You must therefore build up your marketing muscle.

Start by compiling a list of all the people you know that travel and those who can afford to travel but need that extra inspiration.

One successful marketing tool is a newsletter. Create your own newsletter and mail your personalized note to the people you wish to attract.

Depending on your market, the newsletter can be as simple as listing all the bargain air fares to popular destinations or it can be as elaborate as describing a special cruise or recommending a particular tour. You might detail a day-by-day itinerary of a special tour you are promoting.

Include a return coupon to measure the effectiveness of your newsletter. These coupons are available free through the agency you approach.

Contact the employees and the head of the companies to whom you give your personal business - your banker, dentist, doctor, hairdresser, etc. Enlist their business.

Step 3

Teach yourself product knowledge. The brochures are written for the consumer. However, most of the consumers do not want to read piles of pamphlets. It is your job to pass on the information with enthusiasm.

The more you read, the more you learn. The more you learn, the more you sound like an expert. The more you sound like an expert, the more confidence your clients have in you and the more money you will earn.

Product knowledge also speeds up the time spent on a specific transaction. The agent who knows the answer does not have to spend time searching in books for answers to the client's questions. Product knowledge gives you confidence and makes your job more enjoyable.

Instant product knowledge can be gained through studying travel brochures and looking at travel videos. One of the best ways to gain additional knowledge about the products you are selling is to call the sales representative of the product you wish to sell.

Tell the sales representative that you need some help in becoming familiar with the product. Point out to the representative that you are taking the liberty of tape recording all the information, so that you will have the opportunity to listen and learn repeatedly in the privacy of your own car or at home.

Gain product knowledge through practical experience. Practice on yourself by pretending you are the one going on a trip.

For instance, pretend you are flying to Hawaii. Check out all the different flight schedules and the fares different airlines charge. It might just be your luck that the next time a client calls, he will ask for information on a trip you just planned for yourself.

The client will be impressed by all the first-hand information and options you have so readily available.

Step 4

Familiarize yourself thoroughly with all of the trips advertised each week in the local newspaper, plus those in at least one major newspaper on the East Coast and one on the West Coast.

Remember, the stock broker who is too preoccupied to read the Wall Street Journal has skinny kids.

## Step 5

Approach a minimum of two group potentials a month. For your first group interview, you might ask a senior agent to accompany you or invite the sales representative of the product you are attempting to sell to participate in your presentation.

Remember, if you depend on intercepting existing travel, you will be an average agent, but if you create travel, you will go in the hall of fame.

## Step 6

When you deliver your clients' airline tickets, include a brochure featuring a vacation package. The brochure might inspire the client to indulge in a vacation at a famous resort.

## Step 7

If you come across a brochure which arouses your imagination, send it off to a prospective traveler. Brochures are printed for distribution. Make it your daily routine to mail at least one brochure to one of your clients. Call at least one of your clients each day if only to find out if there are any questions regarding the trip you are handling or to tell a client "Hello. I have been thinking about you."

## Step 8

Do not reach a decision on whether or not you should pursue the travel industry unless you have given the industry your absolute best for at least one year, preferably two.

## Step 9

Contribute to the office environment by placing the interests of your co-workers at least as high as your own. Your good relationship with other staff members will increase your productivity and you will learn from them.

## Step 10

Have an intelligent routine. Get the necessary rest in order to have your biological clock perform at its top potential. Keep your body internally clean of any pollutants.

Remember, maximum energy and consistent behavior is needed to fully enjoy your job and to emerge as a winner.

## Step 11

In moments of stress, seize the opportunity to be in command of your personal attitude. Benefit from the increased flow of adrenaline by channeling the natural stimulant into positive ideas that foster success.

## Step 12

Look at a crisis as an opportunity to jet ahead of the crowd by either resolving the crisis or by detecting and acting on the benefit a crisis often carries.

Crises are excellent times for proving your true leadership qualities. Remember, the Chinese ideogram for crisis also carries the character for opportunity. Everything we do in life can have value as long as we learn from it.

## Step 13

Never criticize or qualify a client. Expect the best and you will receive it. Agents who criticize their clients usually lack the art of communicating with the different personalities clients have.

## Step 14

Try to be as enthusiastic as possible. Remember, the trip is to take place at your desk.

Step 15

Keep in mind that success doesn't know any miracles, it only knows hard work. Differentiate yourself from your competitor by offering better service. Differentiate yourself from your colleagues by doing more for the company you work for than they do. And, do more for your clients than anybody else does.

Step 16

Remember your personal success rises in direct relationship with putting other – your partner, your clients, and your co-worker – first. This behavior also will make your company immune against any economic crisis.

Step 17

Have you ever thought of what would happen if you secretly picked the title you want and then worked within the rules of that title? Chances are you soon would wear that title's crown. Just imagine how successful you would be if you were to pretend to be the president of American Express or Director of Marketing or Vice President for Public Relations.

Step 18

Set yourself apart from your competitor by offering better service. Superior service is too many clients far more important than discounted prizes. Try it; you might be surprised.

Differentiate yourself from your colleagues by doing more for the company you work for than they do. And, of course, do more for your clients than anybody else does.

Step 19

Keep in mind that success doesn't know any miracles – it knows only hard work. If you are a novice in the travel industry, scratch the phrase

"No one trained me" from your vocabulary. Winners have success stories; losers have excuses.

Keep in mind this story:

Most of the youth of my German city of Essen where training for the cities important annual athletic competition. To win the 100 meter track race, was more meaningful to me than anything else at that particular time of my critical teenage life.

"You won't make it. You just moved here. You are too new. You haven't trained. You don't even have running shoes to make the team." Those were some of the excuses my friends consoled me with.

But I would not listen. To win I had to out race my cousin, Hildegard, and that was all I could think of. I talked a school mate into letting me borrow her tennis shoes. They were two sizes to large, but, who would know. I surely wasn't about to tell anybody.

With my skinny, short legs ending in my classmates running shoes, I talked my teacher into giving me a chance and at least letting me have a starting spot in the race.

Finally the time came, kneeling at the start, shoulder to shoulder in a straight line with other contenders, I observed and then eagerly adapted to my competitors crouching positions.

Suddenly a shot fired from a gun through the autumn air. My long legged competitors pushed away from the start. Following their lead, I did the same. From that moment on I did not hear, see, or feel anything. Not even the cheers of the crowd pierced my concentration.

Mein Gott – I won!

Suddenly I had thousands of fans and everyone wanted to be my friend. I felt on top of the world.

There is absolutely no feeling that can even come close with the enormous high that fires from victory.

"You run so fast, why we never even saw your feet touch the ground!" my friends told me.

I had a good reason why my feet barely touched the ground, but I was not about to admit to anyone that I had broken a toe inside my friends large running shoes, while pushing away from the start. I had learned early on in life, that winners do not have excuses. Only losers do.

Winning is possible, even without training, or without someone coaching you. Winning takes a desire so strong, that you find your own ways to victory.

Step 20

Be prepared, always thinking ahead. Anticipate the client's questions and be able to offer a pleasing answer.

In today's market, most customers are trained to ask for discounts. Explain to the client who request a rebate that, while your company does not offer discounts, you do provide the best possible service, which includes saving them money up front.


Step 21

Look at recessions, inflations and depressions as the key to new opportunities.

The shopping center which houses one of my offices had an abundance of vacant space. It was breathing heavy under the burden of a recession and was near death. The remaining shops and offices agreed they needed to find a way to attract the public.

I went to the center's management and presented my plan. "Let me have the vacant space next door to my office, and I will run travel extravaganzas. I t will attract consumers to the shopping center. If you find a new tenant for the space I will be out within 30 days."

The center's management was excited and so was I – the rent was free. The place needed a face lift as badly as I did, but businesses almost always comes first.

As I watched the carpenter go over some repairs, the painter brighten up the walls and the janitor clean up the mess, I wondered how to attract consumers to the travel extravaganza in the most effective manner. Perhaps there was even a way to attract travelers free of charge.

Then it came to me – the janitor, the carpenter, and the painter were in daily contact with people who had money. People who were untouched by the present economic crisis.

I asked the facelift team, "What trip would you take if given the oppurtunity?" They looked at me with twinkling eyes.

"A cruise," the janitor quickly said quickly.

"England. I always wanted to show my wife England," said the carpenter with an excited tone in his voice.

The painter dreamed of reliving his "R&R" in Hawaii.

"Your wishes are granted. Here are the conditions," I said. They looked at me in disbelief.

"Make a list. Write down the names and addresses of your clients who take trips. I'd like to invite them to a travel show. If 15 people sign up to any of your dream trips, you earn a free trip."

When they said good-bye that afternoon, I watched them walk across the empty parking lot toward their pick-up trucks. Their walks were much more vigorous than the day before, and their arms were weighted down with travel brochures for their clients. I knew in my heart that, in a few days when I gave my first travel extravaganza, this shopping center would be filled with cars, and that, before the summer was over, a painter, a carpenter, and a janitor would be living their dream trip. I just knew it.

Step 22

A thrifty marketing plan can bring higher returns than a costly one.

One of my colleagues used to spend considerable amounts of money for a large travel extravaganza, but she was dissatisfied with the return. So, this year, she invited just a selected few consumers, and a very charming woman who had written a book and was eager to have public exposure.

The author invited her friends to the travel show. The travel agent bought some of the author's books and offered them as door prizes.

Nearly 100 people came to the travel show/book-signing party. By the end of the evening, 25 people had given their deposit for the Alpine Trip to Europe.

Step 23

Be a character. Set yourself apart from your competitors.

You might write a book or have written one about your company outlining your philosophy. The book could be of great help in having your staff identify with your company.

These are the sure elements for success. Keep in mind that the client has to have an incentive in order to be motivated to award you with the sale.

And, while you are at it, make goals for yourself and give yourself incentives that will motivate you. Make use of the same solid foundation of goals, incentives, and motivations that you will build for your clients and, eventually, for your own employees.

The practice will make you perfect! It will give you insights into the behavior of others which will help you when you work with clients and colleagues, and when you take over the role of leader in your own agency!

Hang on to your enthusiasm and keep learning, I learn something new every day.

**Years later,**
**After Internet, the *Big Bang,* that Changed the Business Climate on**
**the Planet**

Where have all my peers gone? Many of them were most successful in the travel industry. Awe inspiring they were, and so almighty that at national meetings of us travel agents, their very presence intimidated many of us smaller creatures into total submission. They were the dinosaurs in the travel industry, big and powerful. And yet, where are they today?

Maybe they didn't adopt to the ever-changing business climate, feared computerization, or simply resented the Internet, considered it a threat rather than a benefit. Consequently they found themselves left on the side of the road of evolution.

Perhaps they feared the country's political future, listened to political *hopefuls* promise guarantied health insurance for all, higher minimum wages and higher taxes, and calculated that their business could not survive if the country would indeed follow the social example of France and Germany, the country I came from and left for the best country on the planet, the U.S.A.

Lucky me! Here I am, still in the business of planning exciting vacations for interesting people from around the globe. Most of all, continue to love being a travel agent. Honestly, how many professionals do you know who love their job after performing it for nearly 50 years? And how many professionals do you know who's pictures appeared on the front page of their national trade magazine? Well, when I look in the mirror, I see such a person and I blink at myself and whisper, "it pays to be determined. Survivors never give up. Winners always want to learn new tricks."

Unquestionable, I must be doing something right. Clearly, doing a job as well makes us resilient.

Without a doubt, I am on the right track. And I don't mind sharing. That's why I wrote this book. I want you to have the same fabulous life style I have. I want you to see all the fantastic places in the world, and be *nice and be fun.* Let me entertain you with my most recent example.

The airline changed one of our customer's flight schedule. According to the new itinerary, Mrs. Jones now had an eight hour layover in Houston and had to spend the night in a hotel. I called the airline. The uncompassionate agent told me, "Mrs. Jones has to buy a new airline ticket, if she wants a more convenient flight schedule."

Dissatisfied I hang up the phone and called again. It took several calls until finally I struck gold. Already by the new airline representative friendly voice I could tell help was on its way. And yes, Mrs. Jones got exactly what she and I wanted, a great flight schedule at no extra cost. You see we all think we do a great job and we should charge. But do we really? We can all do a better job. We can all be nicer. A smile brings a higher reward than the most expensive stylish suit, and a smile is free. Have a mirror hang by your phone and smile when you talk. Our body language says it all. The sound of our voice is twice as important as our words. Doing something as easy and as much fun as just being nice not only makes a customer or the people around us happy, it also makes us happy.

By the way, Mrs. Jones returned my favor big time. She booked a large wedding party on a cruise ship with our agency, Envoye Travel, which made me smile for weeks.

Today many small business owners and their associates fear the Internet. I don't! They remind me of the workers who feared for their future after the invention of the steam engine. I love the Internet. The Internet is my friend but I also realize that to look into a person's eyes is irreplaceable. Today's statics show that luxury travelers prefer a look into an agent's eye, over a screen.

Maureen from Arizona said, "Many people have the idea that booking a vacation through a travel agency is more expensive. However that is simply not true."

In fact in most cases it is less expensive to book through a professional and it certainly is more fun. Of course, the most important reason why you should book with a travel agent is *service*. On service we travel agents beat the Internet every single time.

The internet is the present and travel will always be the future. To travel is to live.


one last thing
"Walk your way with joy like
the hero on his way to victory"


See you in Botswana!

# Afterword

The inevitable arrived. In 2017 my 50th anniversary. I had to make a heartbreaking decision. Step down and retire and turn Envoye over to the next generation. I was forced to rely on the younger generation to keep Envoye Travel alive. After all Envoye Travel was the oldest agency in our area and the 2nd oldest American Express represented office and I wanted to continue its legacy. I turned to Charly Camp a local real estate agent. Charley told me, "I have never sold a company, but I can certainly try. Someone just sold a stationary store in the small town of Texas to a guy in Hawaii on the internet."

Already, the following week Charly had an appointment for me with Directors Choice. Directors Choice had already been in business for 20 years and operated 80 groups a year. Directors Choice was the perfect fit for Envoye Travel, for one they were local, and secondly they were interested in expanding their operation into leisure travel. It was mutually agreed that our business connection would be the perfect marriage. We contacted American Express and they graciously approved of the bond. Now we are in our first year and John and Amy Lock are the owners of Directors Choice and Envoye Travel and Dilford, my husband, and I could not be any happier, especially since the owners of Directors Choice have given the Envoye Travel staff an option to continue working with them. The latest good news is, they will have a memorial wall reflecting Envoye's exciting and historic past.

The name of Envoye Travel lives on.

I Sigrid, now have the privilege to share my amazing travel adventures with others through books.

Books available:
**Amazing Women**
- The unique adventure of 4 German girls, traveling 25,000+ miles in 18 months, with 0 money
**Chile**
**Peru**
**The Immigrant**
**Short Stories**
**A Christmas Tale for Each Advent Day**
- A book illustrated by children from around the world

Sigrid falling in love with the African Serengeti.

Sigrid jogging on the Great Wall of China.

Ready to celebrate Carnival in Rio.

Christmas in Austria

Floating Airport on the Amazon River. Ready for a ride on the Catalina!

The largest flowers the four German friends had ever received.

Trekking on top of the world. Sigrid lost her
suitcase on the way to Katmandu.

Chiloe has one of the world's highest tides.

The real musher fell off the sled, and I was fast
enough to jump on and put on the brakes.

Among them, two future millionaires.

One of Sigrid's favorite hobbies.

Chilean Patagonia

Waiting on a plane repair.

Sworn in as an official American citizen.

Sigrid and husband, Dilford

Sigrid and friend Anneliese. Annaliese wanted me to become a blonde.

Exploring Mayan temples

Travel Agent Sigrid

Lifelong friendships made through an 18 month trip through South
America. Read the book <u>Amazing Women</u> to find out more!

Tea on the Titanic… on the Hollywood movie set, of course!

Going ashore on an island of Antarctica. Surprise! Who should be the official photographer of the expedition? My pilot from Botswana!

Printed in the United States
By Bookmasters